Community-Oriented Marketing

Community-Oriented Marketing

Marketing

✦

The Definitive Guide To Enlightened Business Development

Ian Bryan

iUniverse, Inc.

New York Lincoln Shanghai

Community-Oriented Marketing
The Definitive Guide To Enlightened Business Development

iUniverse, Inc.

For information address:
iUniverse, Inc.
2021 Pine Lake Road, Suite 100
Lincoln, NE 68512
www.iuniverse.com

Contributing Editor:
Mimi Sandeen

Illustrations, Charts & Diagrams:
Andrew Revere

Author Photo:
Jeff Cravotta

ISBN: 0-595-30881-3

Printed in the United States of America

Contents

Authors Note

Most of the people quoted in this book appear under their own names and tell true stories. In the instances in which people did not wish to be identified, I have referenced them with changes to location, name and sometimes even industry affiliation in order to protect their privacy. It is likely that by the time this book reaches its readers, some of the businesses I have referenced will be closed or in transition. This only re-affirms one of the precepts which spawned this book: that the urban arena is always evolving. The key to staying on track amidst the buzzing business panorama of new information and ideas is to stay alert, open minded and compassionate.

Acknowledgements

Many mentors, friends and clients have contributed over recent years to the professional evolution of Community-Oriented Marketing from an idea in a notebook into a world class method of business development. Alan Brown, Anthony Robbins, Bobbie Huskey, Peggy Douglass and Jeremiah Desmarais were amongst those who offered up the pearls of wisdom and inspiration which set the foundation for this book.

Special thanks to Josephina, Amanda, Kate, Germania, Marcia, Nancy, Pay, Bill, Sara, Theresa, Michelle and all of the artful contributors to our "Writer's Nights" in Chicago. You mean the world to me.

Warm personal thanks to Virginia Waymouth, Talina Gregory, Heather & Sam Pike, Nicole Gregory and Andrew Revere.

Finally, deepest thanks go to my greatest and most inspiring teachers, Zoey Waymouth and Jane Goodall.

Introduction

If you're like me, you're always on the watch for more insights, more information and more opportunities to grow—as a person and as a professional. That's what you'll find in community-oriented marketing. This book details a practical way of doing business that improves our lives, communities and even the greater economics of the cities which make up so much of our changing world. How does it work? Community-oriented marketing is all about manifesting your own growth, while creating growth that works for your people. You do this by rolling up your sleeves and empowering each community to reach their own highest potential and achieve their goals.

While the world around us is changing at lightning-fast speed, the majority of all businesses continue to follow outdated, traditional marketing models. For the smaller business in an urban setting, advertising has become obnoxious, highly expensive and unreliable. We now know that small to medium-sized businesses form the backbone of successful metropolitan economies and ecosystems. And even as small business is experiencing unprecedented growth, many marketers face miniscule budgets to work with. The reality is that traditional marketing is the kiss of death to many of these enterprises, blocking the path to profitable, sustainable business growth. To *survive* in today's world of change, we need an approach that reflects real-world dynamics. To *flourish*, we need an approach that works with those dynamics, and builds into the future. We need something new: something exciting, rewarding and sustainable. We need an innovative, systematic business growth model which is flexible and responsive to the needs of each marketer. Most importantly we need to prove to all generations to follow that socially responsible business works! It offers predictable, highly successful, systematic growth models which we can all follow, regardless of our chosen trade.

So I wrote this book for you, the city-based professional who wishes to move away from the crumbling ecosystem of mainstream traditional marketing, while moving towards an effective and fulfilling method of business development. This book is about generating business in an urban setting by focusing on and empowering local communities. And while Community-Oriented Marketing does work in rural regions, it is because we find the highest number of interconnected communities in metropolitan areas that I have chosen to focus on the urban arena.

That arena is broad and far-ranging, its scope including the greater areas that, like the spokes of a wheel, spread out from the central hub of our cities.

There is currently an intense focus on restoring and redeveloping downtown areas into ideal places in which to live and work and breathe. Art and creativity are experiencing a dramatic rebirth in funding and publicity. Coffeehouses and "people businesses" are popping up in almost irrational proportions all over the country. The people are responding by moving back into inner cities and enjoying their new urban lifestyles. Most importantly, they are building centralized communities which connect with surrounding communities and strengthen civic bonds. At the same time, a growing public disdain for purely economic development and a distrust of large corporations is swelling.

These are the circumstances that, for alert entrepreneurs and professionals, bring community dynamics onto the center stage. The savvy marketer will take advantage of these dynamics by tearing down the dividing wall between business and community. The path to the future—a path they recognize—is in building a creative relationship that supports the needs of community while addressing the needs of business. Building that relationship is what community-oriented marketing is all about.

Before we take that leap, though, a cautionary note—this approach is unlike other marketing model. Please don't confuse it with "Guerilla Marketing" or "Marketing on a Budget." These theories, while valid in certain applications, are responsible for many businesses falling short of their expectations and closing their doors. The difference between this and other models is that community-oriented marketing is holistic: it approaches the marketplace and your business as part of an entire, interconnected social whole. It includes you, the marketer, as a vital and integral part of this dynamic. It's an economic plan, asking practical questions and suggesting practical actions. Yet it also contains the seeds of social action. This is a pro-active paradigm, grounded in good economic sense that grows out of good people sense.

With this in mind, it's important to incorporate as much of this model into your marketing action plan as possible. There are books that can be read with a "take this, leave that" attitude. I've read some of them myself and made good use of them that way. But in this case, it's when the model in its entirety is put in place that you will experience ideal business growth. That means looking at the whole picture and treating it as such. The measure of what you bring to this model is the measure of what you will get out of it, both as a professional and as an individual. And that, too, is holistic.

I have designed this book to serve as a stepping stone for active business and a head-start for new businesses. As community-oriented marketing continues to grow, I am sure that there will be much more to say. That's why I encourage you to visit www.community-oriented.com, where we will focus on keeping the information on current trends up to date. Let me know how it goes. Send an email to ianbryan@community-oriented.com with your stories and ideas about what has worked for you. Thank you.

"You can resist an invading army, but you cannot resist an idea whose time has come."

—Victor Hugo

PART I
The Staging Ground

Take A Lesson From The Nonprofits

In April of 2000, I began consulting in a developmental capacity for various non-profit organizations. About 6 months after the events which took place on September 11th, 2001 had impacted America's economy, I noticed that many of the nonprofit organizations which continued to grow, despite major cutbacks in funding, were the ones who made up for that funding through donations from the community. While many nonprofit organizations were forced to close their doors, some actually *grew faster*. What really surprised me was that well-planned fundraising events, especially those which attracted families, drew larger attendance than ever before.

The reasons why quickly grew obvious. The events of September 11th had impacted *all* of American life, generating responses in one area that were then felt in other areas, including the economic. After September 11, people began to focus more on their families and on connecting with people whom they cared about. For the nonprofits which made themselves cornerstones of the PEOPLE communities, there was continued support. For the nonprofits which had focused most of their developmental attention on BUSINESS communities and grant funding, there was vast disappointment. In this model, we have nonprofit organizations which choose to focus on large chunks of income, funneled through several forms of business, government and civic organizations.

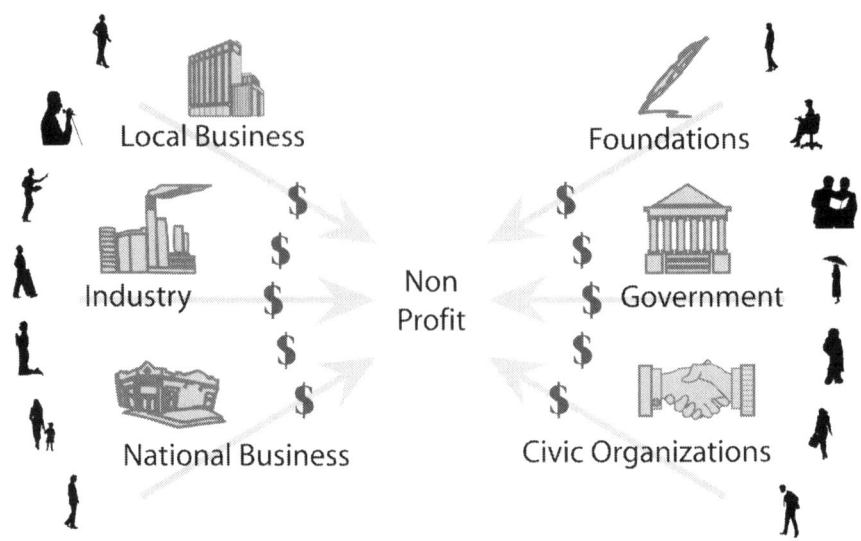

For the nonprofits which made themselves cornerstones of BOTH BUSI-NESS AND PEOPLE communities, there was the highest degree of success and comfort in those difficult times. In this model, we have nonprofit organizations which choose to focus on vast community support by connecting directly with the community.

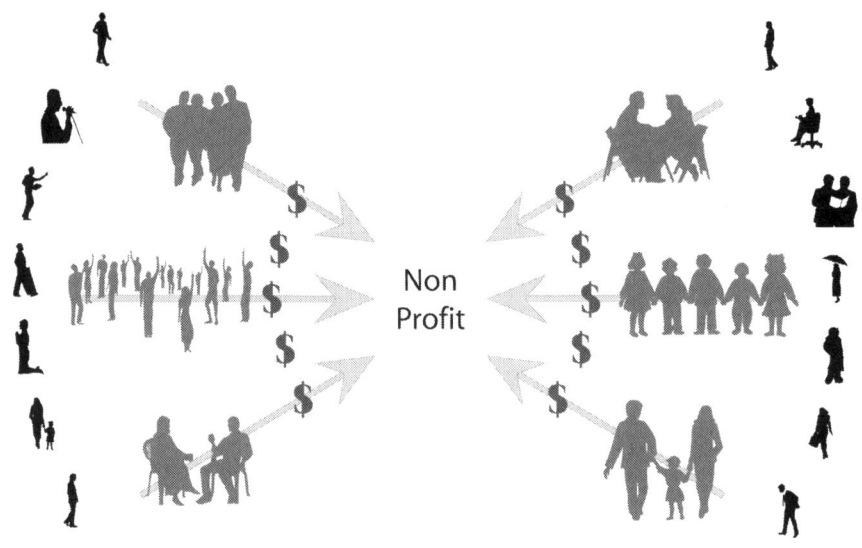

The association between successful fundraising and direct community involvement was demonstrable. The link was not just in the deeds of these nonprofits, but also in the perception connected to their deeds. In working with these organizations, I recognized that in order for a nonprofit to build a strong, supportive community, its message and activities in the community must achieve at least one of the following:

1. It must be perceived as an institution which is necessary to the positive workings of society (literacy projects, shelters, free clinics, humane societies, etc), or

2. It must be perceived by the public as making an essential contribution to an enhanced quality of living (performing arts, nature conservatories, historical societies, etc).

This was a significant observation, one that put my own consulting work with nonprofits into perspective. But then came the bigger connection—*the business connection*. I'll never forget the day I first made it, while in the midst of reviewing my notes for a client as I sat in a coffee shop in Southaven, Mississippi. Have *you* made the connection already? If not, go back and reread the last few paragraphs and replace the word "nonprofit" with the words "for profit."

The Story Of The Sensible City

The client happened to be one of my nonprofits—a professional dance company in Atlanta, Georgia. I had been working around the clock, generating playbill advertising sales for them. Seeking advice, I got into a lengthy conversation with Todd Williams, the owner of an automobile dealership from my home town. Todd told me that he *only* advertised by means of nonprofit sponsorship. I asked him how he could compete with the many other dealers in town, who spent a bundle on advertising. "Don't have to compete," he said. "People who read the ads in the paper go from dealer to dealer looking for the best price. People who come to me are ready to do business. They feel like they know me because we have something in common from the beginning."

The thing "in common" that Todd spoke of was the support of a common cause. Todd had been ingeniously self-marketing his organization to the community for decades. Inspired, my very next phone call was to another automobile dealership. The young woman who answered the phone was very friendly until she found out that I wanted to sell advertising for a nonprofit. So many businesses are bombarded by organizations begging for a handout that they often lose interest in anything that has to do with the nonprofit community. She quickly dispensed with my call, providing me with the name of their advertising agency.

"No problem," I thought. "I'll just phone up the agency and send them a media kit. In fact, while I'm at it, I think I'll contact every marketing firm in town." To me, this made sense. I knew that those who advertised by sponsoring performing arts (provided that their target market matched the audience) were receiving superior results for less money than the cost of mainstream media advertising. It seemed like a natural. Two months later and after hundreds of phone calls, I had not received a single response from the 17 marketing agencies I had contacted. I turned over my program advertising leads to another consultant and decided to focus purely on development activities.

But it was during this time that I kept turning over an exciting idea. **What if** there was a professional organization that taught businesses, entrepreneurs, nonprofit organizations and civic leaders how to build a deeper sense of community by finding ways in which each element could help the other? After all, aren't the most enjoyable cities in America the ones in which the performing arts are supported, the social services are strong, the small businesses are thriving, the leaders are trusted and over all, there is a sense of interconnectedness in the community? **What if** community empowerment activities and nonprofit awareness were the main events of a business marketing campaign? **What if** I could teach nonprofits and other social organizations how to understand, attract and work hand-in-hand with community-oriented businesses?

"Wouldn't fly," said the little devil in my right ear. "Businesses are married to traditional marketing, our culture is addicted to mass media and besides, how could it possibly work financially?" So many of us have great ideas, but never take action to turn those ideas into viable dreams. I nodded at my little epiphany, enjoyed the fantasy of what *could* happen, and then wrote my idea down in a journal with no intention of ever turning it into a plan. At the time I was so immersed in corporate systems that the notion of bringing a neighborhood connectedness element into the whole of a mainstream urban community seemed impossible.

Still, the idea percolated in the background, tenaciously holding on in my imagination. It had grabbed me somewhere in the gut of my own deepest-held beliefs and hopes and wouldn't let go. Finally, months later and despite my doubts, I got up the nerve to give it a try. In the summer of 2002, I moved with my family to Asheville, North Carolina (in my opinion, one of the greatest cities in the world), where I created a full spectrum marketing service, including a small link on my website for community-oriented marketing. I named my business The Sensible City because creating just that was my goal. I chose Asheville because it offered a classy, thriving downtown area dominated by small businesses and entrepreneurs. In my vision, I knew that if we could get 100 businesses marketing themselves by empowering the community, such an achievement would mean far more than just growth for the businesses involved. It would mean more financial support for education and public health. It would mean more exposure and freedom for the arts. It would mean a series of small improvements that would culminate into a dramatic change in the quality of life for my host city. Asheville became, in a way, a very personal testing ground in which I could play out my vision of a marketing approach that was both sensible and heartful.

Even so, I was not fully committed in the beginning, largely because I had not seen any real results. It was hard to sell the idea of community-oriented marketing. Despite my excitement, I had to confess to my clients that, in the beginning, I was, in fact, offering an *experiment*—one that could potentially cost them money. For the first few months, my small staff and I designed logos, built websites and entertained businesses which, as the little voice in my ear had originally predicted, were only interested in traditional marketing. After several months of this, I was professionally bored.

Fortunately, it was at this time that I met Anne Alexander, a professional life coach, who became so excited about the concept of community-based business growth tactics, she started telling people about it on her own. Anne and I attended the same business networking lunch group, and each time I would see her, she'd say something like, "You really need to push the community thing, Ian." Or, "I think that the community-oriented marketing is going to work." After about a month of Anne's regular support, I talked it over with my partner and made a committed decision. I would focus on the community-oriented marketing concept. If it failed, I would give up business and go back to nonprofit work.

The next morning I sat down at my computer and re-wrote our mission statement and goals to reflect a purely community-oriented business platform. Later the same week, like a voice from the sky, The Sensible City got its first call for a marketing plan based on a purely community-centered approach. The following week, two more businesses requested proposals. We quickly had to convert a great idea into an organized, systematic approach. From that point forward, the business poured in like I have never witnessed any business growth before. As I write this book, The Sensible City has a 3-week waiting list for new business. Through community-oriented marketing, we've now ushered in tremendous growth for restaurants, architects, trade shows, ISP's, bookstores, chiropractors, coffeehouses, catering companies, clothing stores, feng shui consultants, psychic consultants, computer training centers, musicians, couriers, hair salons, real estate offices, IT consulting firms, financial planning firms, outdoor centers, grocery stores, publishing companies, fine artists, galleries, professional speakers, travel agencies, rising politicians and more. With the exception of a few bad apples, we've had only positive results. And now that the results are in, the answer is clear: Community-oriented marketing is much more than an option. It is a must-do for any business operating in an urban setting.

Getting Down To It

The community-oriented marketing model that The Sensible City uses is what this book is all about. This book will teach you how to:

- Grow faster, work smarter, increase sales and retain long-term business relationships by establishing strong, reliable, endeared communities that want to see you grow.

- Open doors to established communities through effective networking with like-minded civic groups, nonprofit organizations, community interest groups and fellow community-oriented business networks.

- Leverage these community relationships for maximum visibility with the press through cross promotions, active sponsorship, community awareness events, nonprofit fundraisers, educational forums and volunteer support.

- Move away from the crumbling ecosystem of mainstream advertising and marketing, while moving towards a sustained state of enlightened business growth through meaningful interactions with the community.

- Spend less money on marketing, while attracting more business per marketing dollar than any other method available today.

- Participate in a method of business development that strengthens urban economies by keeping local money circulating, rather than giving unnecessary handouts to conglomerated media corporations.

Attraction Rather Than Promotion

But to work with this model successfully, you must first have an awareness of the fundamental dynamic underlying it. This is where the lessons of this book truly begin:

This form of marketing is based on attraction rather than promotion. If you aren't already familiar with it, the Law of Attraction basically states: *"That which is alike unto itself is drawn."* So, for instance, those who want to know more about this law and its applications in business will naturally draw this book to them. In picking up this book, you are acting 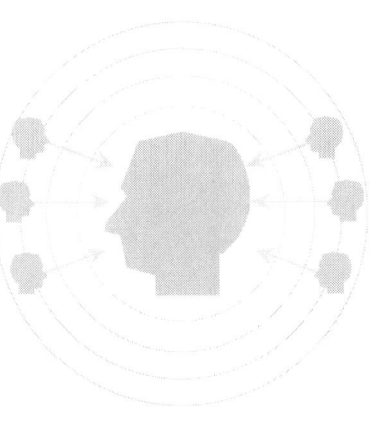 on your own openness to the ideas and the opportunities it holds for you. It may not be immediately apparent to you, but this is the law of attraction in action. And although it may be a subtle notion to you now, it will become more and more evident as you see it play out time and again throughout the pages ahead. Seeing it at work in your own life is an easy transition to make. And that's the necessary transition you must make in order to reap the benefits of what this book has to offer.

If you are familiar with the personality characteristics and strengths of your target audience, you may already be enacting this law. For example, I know a woman with a consulting practice whose ideal customers are "professionals who believe in socially responsible business and value diversity and progressive thinking." They are honest, community-minded and environmentally sensitive. These are her ideal clients because that's who she is. That's what she believes and that's what she puts out into the world by enacting a business model which expresses those principles each day.

Remember the "bad apples" I mentioned before? The Sensible City has issued refunds and closed files on several client accounts. Sales-minded, over-hungry business owners and executives who attempt to exploit this system purely for personal gain will fail in every attempt at community-oriented marketing. Whether driving a bargain at a charity ball or faking an affinity for children in order to tap into the family market, insincere businesses are not welcomed by independent communities. I have even heard of a nonprofit organization that issued a donor a refund and asked that they peddle their product somewhere else. Another way to look at the law of attraction: your action and your intention are Siamese Twins, joined at the hip. Where one goes, so goes the other. But it's not a one-way movement. It's a complete cycle—whatever you put out comes back to you.

Keep in mind that, just as cynicism begets its own cynical response, so to do positive and sincere actions produce positive responses. To truly play out the law of attraction in business development, you must recognize that you are growing your business by empowering others. Inherent in the act of giving is the humbling of the self and a detachment from results. What this means is that while your overall marketing plan is carefully measured and formulated for maximum growth, your *behavior* while working with the community must be sincere and entirely detached from a sales approach. Later in this book, we'll talk about producing results without being married to them.

It's All In The Heart

Barry Potekin lost most of his money in bad investments. But his comeback business was the most successful venture of his lifetime career. The founder of Chicago's highly successful Gold Coast Dogs restaurant chain, Potekin donates $10,000 annually to various Chicago homeless shelters and about $15,000 each year to the Make-A-Wish Foundation. He's known as an influential speaker who offers his gift of motivational influence to students in Northwestern University's MBA program. He's also known for offering young drug addicts in recovery hope by addressing them personally. The question is, why does everybody love Barry? Is it because he donates lots of cash each year? Or is it because he gets involved in the community?

Teaching you how to make your city into a better place for all people, while creating abundance for yourself in the process, is my main purpose in writing this book. Because it works better than any other, this marketing model will sweep America and concurrently, improve the way that we do business across the country. The ideas presented in this book are not new to the marketplace. The strategies, tips and tools have all been used before. The difference is a shift of focus. Community-oriented marketing means bringing out the best in you. It means recognizing your role as a leader by the mere fact that you operate a business which profits from a community. The absence of compassion in the marketplace and workplace is the missing link in our capitalistic economies. Your job, as a business operating with a community-oriented agenda, is to tear open your chest and place your heart out on the table and in so doing, experience tremendous growth. Personal Involvement. Personal Commitment. Real results in the real world.

Are you ready for the road which lies ahead? The three determining questions I set forth for all of my clients are:

1. "Do you believe that you are capable of conducting business in a manner that will make your city and, on a larger scale, the world a better place?"

2. "Can you cultivate the time needed and social skills necessary for you to get out into the community?"

3. "Is your product or service in any way destructive to society as a whole?"

The correct answers are yes, yes and no. Do you qualify? I expect that for most of us reading this book, the answer is yes. So buckle your seatbelt, and let's go visit The Sensible City.

"…a well-connected individual in a poorly connected society is not as productive as a well-connected individual in a well-connected society."

—Robert Putnam in *Bowling Alone*

PART II
Doing Business
In The City

Welcome To The Sensible City

Imagine that you have just arrived in the ideal city. By ideal, I mean **your definition of ideal**. Is it a village in Italy? Is it Paris? Chicago? Does it even exist? Whether real or imaginary, get an idea of what your ideal city is and let's take a quick tour. What do the streets look like? What kinds of sounds and smells fill the air? Check into the ideal hotel, leave your bags in the room and let's walk down Main Street through the center of town. It is late afternoon, the restaurants and bars are preparing for dinner and people are mingling about. As we stroll through town, notice the types of businesses we pass. Take in the activity. Where do people congregate? What appeals to them, and to you?

In my ideal city, there are apartments above the storefronts and people who have a sense of pride about their home town. They are sitting on park benches, window shopping with friends, jogging and riding bicycles. People who live in the same neighborhood know each other and wave at friends in passing. The public library is one of the biggest buildings downtown. Sidewalk musicians are set up every few blocks. Overall, there is a pleasant hum of creativity pulsing through the streets. Up ahead we see a café with tables on the sidewalk. Let's sit down, order something tasty and watch the people go by as the evening sets in.

For most of us, the ideal city does not exist outside of our imaginations. This is unfortunate. It explains why so many Americans rarely leave their suburban environments and venture into downtown areas. Certain elements may exist in different cities and you may even know of a city that is 95% ideal. But ideal is never found if you look at the big picture. Whether it is the presence of racial tension, soulless corporations dominating every block, environmentally insensitive development, extreme poverty and class segregation, the lack of anything fun to do in town or even just those guys on loud Harley Davidsons that rip your ears out each time they take off from a red light, finding the perfect city could be a lifelong endeavor.

But a piece of your ideal city is found in every urban center on earth. And while we all have different opinions about what specifically makes a city ideal, I have found that there is one thing in common that most every city-minded individual wants: a culturally rich, community-centered downtown which offers its inhabitants a higher quality of life. By this I mean music, dance, theatre and other fine arts, small businesses, street festivals, independent bookstores, plentiful information resources, abundant social services and more. All of these resources are made possible by people enacting their dreams with the support of their respective communities.

Your city, the place where you do business, is the ultimate playing field where all of these things come together. When you have dinner with friends in a restaurant, buy tickets to the show or go shopping with your spouse, you are participating in an interconnected web that affects every single human being involved. Within this interconnected web are the resources by which people define their quality of life.

This understanding is essential to engaging in community-oriented marketing. I make a strong point of it because so many of us feel cut off and isolated from the people around us. An interesting little study that was produced in 1999 by New Human, Inc. showed that while dining at a restaurant in your home town next to a table of people you have never met, the distance from complete strangers to finding strong points in common is found in an average of 3 questions. The results of this study are the reason why I never discuss sensitive business matters that are not supposed to be public while eating at a packed sushi bar. Have you ever met someone you thought you had no connection to at all and within a few minutes of conversation, it turned out that you had major contacts or important places in common?

Whether or not you acknowledge this interconnectedness, it is always there. Not long ago, I had the privilege of sharing a table with Cheri Britton, an educator and speaker in Asheville, North Carolina. We were talking about self-made businesspeople and self-made millionaires. Cheri's opinion on this subject inspired me to rethink my own. She said that "there is no such thing as a self-made businessman, millionaire, or any other individual." This conversation still pops into my mind on a regular basis. When I look back on the big breaks in my own life, I see nothing but people opening doors. Granted, I sought those people out. But we are all made with the support, inspiration and resources of other people.

If you wish to succeed in community-oriented marketing, you must know people and you must understand who they are, where they go, what they want and why they want it. Knowing people means knowing your city. Walk around, meet business owners and eat in every single restaurant that is open to the public. While you're at it, talk to your waiter, salesperson or cab driver. Talk to everybody! Attend lectures and art showings, book signings and other exhibitions. Get involved in every scene with appeal. Once you decide which communities you are going to get involved in, commit yourself to truly getting involved—go to as many social events as possible and read the newsletters. Find out who is making tracks in politics and watch for their social web.

And once you make that commitment, don't hold back. One thing that I ask of you and of every client I work with is that you hold yourself to the highest and most generous standards of social contact. Much of community-oriented marketing is based on your appreciation and support of local organizations that are currently active in your target market's community. Offer your support and donate your time as a volunteer. As much as you can, get involved in people's lives. When you meet directors and executives (who could easily refer you enormous amounts of business), ask them what you can do to support them beyond just sponsoring.

Becoming A Hero
In The Community

Most cities have a cultural foundation which offers its inhabitants the resources by which they define a high quality of life. Those resources, as I've mentioned, vary greatly—from educational strongholds to neighborhood watch groups; from sophisticated professional dance companies to down-to-earth coffeehouses; from an abundance of music to a plethora of public street fairs. What these resources all hold in common are the people—the people who bring them into existence; the people who support them; the people who attend them. In essence, the guts of what makes our cities thrive are the people who come together to bring life to every populated urban landscape in town.

When a group of people get together and decide to do so with any degree of recurrence, they form what we often stuff into a catch-all term: community. In most cases, a community will only endure if nurtured by a common cause, the distribution of information or inspiration, a pleasurable social dynamic, a major location in common, and/or in most cases, a committed organization through which the common cause is represented. The term community can apply to a group of four friends who hang out regularly or it can apply to an entire city of 13 million. But for the purpose of this book, in definable community, there is something beautiful which happens. People come together and find a common ground by which they associate. They share resources, make friends and support each other personally. At the same time, sustainable communities are often populated by members who draw upon each other's strengths to get an important job done.

In any community, there are leaders and there are heroes. Most members of the community know who they are. They are the facilitators, the motivators, the nurturers, the movers and the shakers. They are the ones we turn to for advice or for aid in times of challenge. They are the men and women we hold in our sight as the models that we aspire to in politics or in business, in the arts, sports or education. They galvanize our imaginations as they focus and drive our community spirit.

We all need leaders. The groups of people who comprise our communities are always looking for more icons to inspire them, to do for them what they believe they cannot do for themselves. Your job, as a business owner or marketing executive, is to brand your business by becoming a hero in the community. By your presence, through your deeds, you can create a focal point for the kind of change and action that people and their communities thrive on. This is the presence that is felt and acknowledged by those people—your marketplace.

You've seen business at work in the community. Those of us who live in areas with the Trader Joe's line of grocery stores, for instance, know that Trader Joe's champions the protection of the environment and endangered species. In fact, the first time I ever visited a Trader Joe's was in response to their call to an endangered species rescue facility I was volunteering at. They telephoned to offer us a donation of salads and green vegetables to use as feed. Since then, I have spent thousands of dollars in their stores across the country.

Take a look at the many ways businesses have been opening community doors. A business can even grow a heroic reputation out of the good deeds of its employees. This means *any* person working in that company—not just the corporate board members—can have the power to extend entrepreneurial caring into their community. The Starbuck's Foundation rewards and encourages all employees to find volunteer projects in their communities. As an incentive, the foundation gives generous grants to organizations where Starbuck's employees volunteer. Sonapress Incorporated has annual incentive programs for employees who choose to give each week to the United Way. These businesses are a force for good because they empower organizations that empower!

You don't have to be a large corporation to make a huge difference. The examples I cited above go beyond standard giving. Millions of dollars are distributed each year by corporations who simply write checks in exchange for a promotional opportunity. This is great, and I warmly congratulate them, but writing checks is not a necessary cornerstone of community-oriented marketing. In fact, making donations is often counter-productive. Patagonia, a national outdoor clothing & gear company, has donated over $18 million to environmental groups since the mid 1980's. But what affiliate this national brand with environmental conservation are the activities by which they create awareness for and foster volunteer communities. Each year Patagonia measures a tangible result and reports back to the community. They are amongst the most expensive brands in the outdoor industry, yet despite concerns about decreased consumer spending, they are still growing strong.

For the small business owner, it may intimidate you to read about big corporate brands and what they are doing in terms of community-oriented marketing. But you needn't worry: this book is based on my experience, which is primarily with a small to medium-sized business community. You'll find plenty of examples in the coming chapters of small businesses engaged in similar projects. The best part is that as a small business, your activities will likely get more attention than your big biz competitors. And as for the marketing executives of big companies—don't be put off by my affection for small business. As I mentioned before, community-based marketing has worked for some of the greatest brands on earth. As is the microcosm, so is the macrocosm.

As I said before, your city is your marketplace. You are learning how to do business in a way that will turn your marketplace into a stronger, more sustainable community. By putting these methods into practice, you become a responsible citizen, a compassionate leader and a force for good.

Understanding Our Changing Inner Cities

The obvious question behind marketing for the last 50 years has been, "What do people want?" More specifically, for the purpose of focusing on doing business in an urban economy, "What do people in our cities want?" And that leads us right to the core question: "Where are our cities going?" Lately, the picture in American cities is vastly different than it was just 10 years ago.

1. An unstoppable movement is on, led by civic leaders, to strengthen our inner cities and develop them into clean, safe, enjoyable meccas in which to live and visit.

2. Amidst this resurgence of inner-city economic activity, the top 50 cities in America now account for 25% of new jobs, but only 16% of the population.

3. After decades of declining civic life, we see a new surge in community participation organizations across the country. Based on an NHI 2001 population study, 3 out of every 5 Chicagoans working and living within 3 miles of city center were involved in at least one community service organization besides church. Half of those involved in regular community-serving activities held responsible positions or roles within those organizations.

4. A rising class of health-minded, spiritually sensitive, environmentally conscious citizens (many with disposable incomes) who possess a cross-cultural affinity for community involvement are making their homes within 5 miles of urban centers.

5. A dramatic public outcry has finally emerged against the "corporatization" of our urban centers. So many of us who do rely on corporate chains resent them. We are losing our culture—losing our identity to the businesses to which, for some reason, we seem addicted. In response,

more and more cities are developing buildings and districts which only permit local merchants to open shop.

6. In his excellent book, *The Rise of the Creative Class*, Richard Florida details how we now stand witness to a global shift in which more than 30% of our nation's workforce belong to the creative community, with the majority of them living and working in our cities. With this as optimistic fuel, competitive cities are already recognizing and catering to an economy that is fired by creativity.

In order to stay focused on community-oriented marketing, I am only citing the urban transitions which reflect upon the subject matter at hand. There are many other developments happening in our cities which I encourage you to explore. For a list of educational books and resources on our changing cities, check out www.community-oriented.com.

Making Sales In The Sensible City

Now that we have a basic notion—the lay of the land—of the urban scene, let's get down to the "how" of generating sales. For openers, we know that in business, relationships are more important for maintaining residual income than are hard sales. For some, this confuses the nature of selling. From a community-oriented marketing perspective, the process of selling falls into two stages. Act One, The Introduction. Act Two, The Experience. Then comes the Encore, which we will talk about later.

Before we get started, let's set the stage. Ask yourself this question: After you see an outstanding movie, performance or show, do you tell others about it? Absolutely. Why? Because you have experienced something special that you wish to share with others. We all know that it is by word of mouth that ideas, good books, new restaurants, great theatre shows, hot news topics and other information/entertainment venues experience tremendous growth. So how can we apply this to your business?

ACT ONE: THE INTRODUCTION

In today's urban business marketplace, more and more goods and services are introduced through three interrelated channels: community recognition & support, referrals from within the consumer's social group and the public perception of professional integrity. Take also into account that, as most marketing classes and books still teach, for the best results, your product should be introduced in a manner which separates it from the competition. And while branding through traditional marketing still dominates introductions in our country, we find that more and more corporations are bragging in their commercials about their commitment to the environment or to specific communities. Banking institutions advertise themselves as your friends; pharmaceutical companies want to make you happy; insurance companies want to be a good neighbor. These companies have figured out that appealing to community values is highly profitable.

In 1999, I was shopping for real estate in Chicago. Rather than contact an agent, I resorted to hunting down listings in the classified advertising section of the newspaper. Each time I would schedule a viewing, I was bombarded by an over-excited real estate agent who wanted to be my pal and show me every apartment in town. Then one day while attending a fundraiser for The Human Rights Campaign, I met Alisha Paine. Alisha told me that she was a broker with a small, 2 person real estate firm. We instantly hit it off and I never spoke to another real estate company in town. Alisha could have been the worst broker in town, but we had an important cause in common. That meeting ground created instant trust.

Years ago I had a business which would buy a tent and sponsor a team at The American Cancer Society's "Walk & Roll Chicago." This is a really fun event wherein most of our employees signed up to either walk 3 miles or bicycle 5 miles in honor of a loved one who has battled cancer. Each person raises at least $100 by asking friends for a donation. When I was signing up David, one of the riders in my group, I was amazed to see that he had obtained a one thousand dollar contribution. Wow! Immediately, I looked to see who made that donation. It was an attorney whose office was just 2 blocks away from my home. I asked David about the attorney, because I was in need of one who handled tax law. Sure enough, his attorney ended up representing me a week later.

Let's imagine for a moment that you are new in town. You are interested in getting in shape and could use a gym and personal trainer. While you are participating in a nonprofit event for an organization you joined as a volunteer, you meet a fellow volunteer who is sponsoring that event. It turns out that he/she is a personal trainer and that he/she offers a discount at the nearby gym he/she is partnered with. Best of all, you both are crazy about the work that this nonprofit you have volunteered for is doing in the community. Are you going to open the phone book and get competing offers or are you instantly going to start working out? For most people, the connection is instant because you immediately have strong values in common. I call customers who come to businesses because of shared values **"Values Partners."** We'll talk more about Values Partners, the best customer that any business can have, throughout this book.

Act One is about finding ways in which you can introduce yourself to your ideal customer by empowering the community of which they are a part. By getting involved, even in the smallest and simplest ways, you are empowering what matters to them. Act One is not just about getting involved with nonprofits, either. Chiropractors get involved in running clubs, even going so far as to create their own. Grocery stores invite the police and neighborhood associations in to do kid ID cards and fingerprinting. I could compile a list of examples a mile long. So just ask yourself: "How can I make introductions within the community which appeal to the values and lifestyles of my ideal market?"

ACT TWO: THE EXPERIENCE

Goods and services must be sold in a manner which feeds an emotional experience to a committed buyer. I choose to put my little boy in organic, chlorine free, biodegradable diapers. Every time I buy diapers, I cringe at the cost (30-45% more than the mainstream brands). But I buy them because I want to experience a *feeling* of caring for the environment. I also want to *know* that I am a *part of* a special generation that associates more value with being responsible than with having extra cash.

Pine and Gilmore's outstanding business book *The Experience Economy* demonstrates how professional services oriented, retail and restaurant businesses take experiential selling to a high level. Themed restaurants, for instance, sell food, but people visit them because they want an experience. Every time you eat out, you dine on an experience. If you walk into a shopping mall and pay attention, you will see more and more retailers are selling an experience, with the product as a prop and the service as a stage. Some might argue that what I am really talking about is nothing more than *adding value* to the product. While this is true in a limited sense, a focus on simply adding value is not enough. Everyone wants to add more value to their product or service. What I am talking about is adding value to the *experience of selecting, buying or making good use of* the product (rather than adding value to the product itself). I am not the first to make this point, but I would like to drive it in. In the future, the key to taking charge in the business world is determined by your ability to create an emotional, empowering and memorable *experience*.

I recently discovered Tim Sanders, Chief Solutions Officer at Yahoo, Inc. and the author of *Love Is The Killer App*. Tim caught my attention because he's hip, he's savvy and his book resonates with my philosophy of doing business. Tim made a presentation in 2000 entitled "Welcome To the Experience Economy." In this lecture, he makes a great example of the importance of creating an experience in order to sell a product by telling a generational story of birthday parties in his family. "When my Mom was a little girl, her birthday was celebrated in a commodities economy," he begins. "Her mom took flour, sugar, water and egg and in a half a day, heated the whole house up for a buck." Sanders goes on to the next generation, where for $2, you could buy cake mix and have the whole thing ready in less than an hour. In the next generation (enter the services economy), all that was needed was a call to the bakery and for $10, voila, the cake with no effort at all. In his humorous conclusion, Sanders states the truth of today's economy, which is that cake is to be expected. Now, if a parent wants to make a child happy, they must stage an experience. This often means skating parties, Celebration Station, Chucky Cheese, Disney World or some other means of interactive, memorable fun.

But what about a service? What if you don't sell a product? That's even easier. Jeremiah Desmarais, CEO of Extremely Graphic Marketing in Chicago & Montreal, is famous for his ability to create a personality sale (i.e., an experience). He's funny, energetic and full of concrete knowledge. When you visit his Gold Coast marketing agency and discuss the prospect of working together, he gives away free (and brilliant) advice. He shoots straight to the bottom line, while cracking you up with industry-relevant jokes. He fills the table with more ideas than your mind can handle. He talks seriously about your goals and applies his vast knowledge of personal growth to every business growth plan. Then he coaches you to lay out your goals and set a schedule for measuring results. He never asks whether or not you want to do business with him. Instead, he offers a celebration. Then you have a choice: you can take all of these unformed ideas and your goals timeline home to mull over, or you can get started.

We follow a similar model at The Sensible City. I have found that the greatest gift I can offer any potential client is a clear vision of where they want to go, what it will take to get there and by what series of actions. What makes this so notable a gift? Take a look at the observations made by David Allen in *Getting Things Done*, his exceptional book about stress-free productivity. Throughout, he constantly revisits the fact that most business owners and executives are so busy and so overwhelmed that they rarely realize what it is that they ought to be doing at any given quiet moment.

Giving the gift of direction, a clear outcome, specific action items and a practical timeline is the experience we offer at The Sensible City before money is ever exchanged. Is there risk involved? Are we giving away too much? Absolutely not. In almost every single case wherein we provide this service to a potential client who does not sign up, that client has referred us other business that did. Why? Because clarity about what to do next relieves stress and replaces it with energetic optimism. To be stress-free is nice, but to be confident and optimistic about a clear, defined future is priceless. And that's an experience that stands out, stays with our potential client, and, one way or another, comes back to us as future business.

But you don't have to get complicated. I recently read about a carwash that got free coverage in the Boston Globe when it was discovered that the business offered free 15 minute chair massages by local therapists for customers who were waiting for their cars to be cleaned. Act Two is about delivery. People want pleasure out of anything that they choose to do. In many cases, a traditional sales approach offers a little bit of fun. But deliver a positive, emotional experience they will always remember, and you've got a stronger chance than anyone else in town of making the sale. Do you remember what I said earlier about word of mouth business growth? It's with this kind of referral that we see the most impressive benefits of combining a sincere, values-based introduction with an experiential product delivery. As the curtain falls, audience satisfaction is what makes the sale.

THE ENCORE

Here's the best part. In the end, it doesn't even matter if you win the sale. If you have followed this sales model so far, you should still have an individual who has experienced something positive and memorable. Hopefully that experience was backed by a values—based introduction. Regardless of the sale, you have just created a special business relationship. Yet, it never ceases to amaze me how many businesses will drop all communication with people who choose not to buy. It further astonishes me how many businesses do not capitalize on their existing customer base. This is a critical mistake, one that will lose you future business. In community-oriented marketing, it is the relationship after the sale (or no-sale) that is the most important.

Last summer, the proprietors of a computer training center contacted my office and requested a marketing consultation. Upon meeting with them, I found that they were in a classic situation: they needed marketing but had overspent their budget. They weren't able to justify the expense of hiring The Sensible City. But before I left, I chose to spend an extra hour at their facility and offered them some ideas and solutions to try on their own. We mapped out monthly goals for three months into the future and I shared some insights with them about ways to gain press in the local newspaper.

I know many businesspeople who shriek in horror at this behavior. "Your time is too valuable for that kind of waste," one of my old business partners would tell me. But less than a month later, I heard back from the co-owner of the training center. They had put an idea that I offered into practice. As a direct result, they had received great press from it, along with dozens of phone calls. Business was picking up and they ended up paying my company to do more work for them. As well, they were quick to tell others about their experience with us.

Remember the Law of Attraction? Take a moment now to think about that dynamic, and apply it to what happened here. A little freely given advice of a way to create business was used by a company ready to do just that. Then, the business they created with that advice brought them back to The Sensible City, ready for more and with the resources to pay for it. Mutual attraction. Mutual satisfaction.

Learn to recognize this dynamic. It underlies the action in Act One and Act Two, and it sustains The Encore. Whatever you put out, including your intention and your desire, will somehow ripple back to you. It did for training center. And it did for The Sensible City. It will work the same way for you.

There are many ways to deliver an encore. What's more, if you practice it right, the encore can last for years and is guaranteed to deliver more business to your door. For a successful, sustained encore, practice the following steps with everyone who experiences your business first hand:

1. Find out what they want/need and **share resources**.

2. **Refer them** to other community-oriented businesses that you trust.

3. **Be a good neighbor** and invite them to stay in touch. Send thanks & greeting cards.

4. Find out what their community affiliations are and see if you can **get involved**.

5. Call them up every 3 to 6 months and **ask specifically for referrals**.

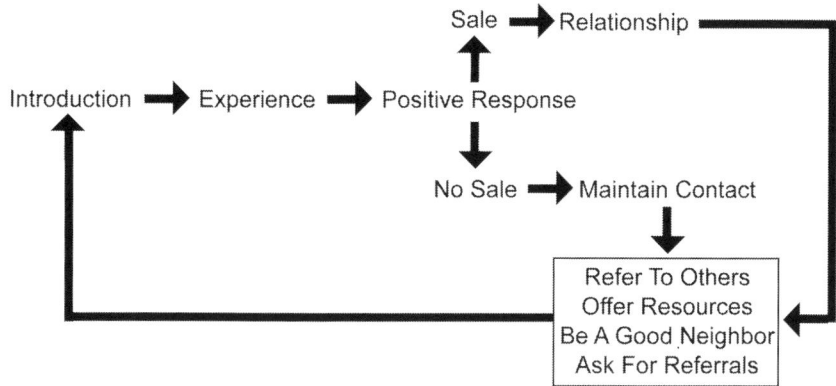

Figure 1.1: Making Sales

If your business is a coffeehouse or a gas station, the encore is less sensible to pursue through business communication tactics. However, the act of respecting and nurturing your audience remains equally important for anyone in business today. So before you move on to the next section, please do yourself a favor. Put down this book, grab a pen and paper, and make a draft plan of how you can rocket launch your business by following these steps. Here are a few questions to keep in mind as you plan out your own Encore for success:

1. What communities possess my target market?
    (Later in this book, we'll consider some important questions you must ask yourself in identifying your target market. If you are unclear of your target market, consider working with a marketing-experienced business coach to find clarity.)

2. What are some creative ways that I can make a difference or get involved with these communities?

3. Upon making introductions, what are some ways that I can develop an emotional, compelling and memorable experience when offering my product or service?

4. After the experience, how can I leverage that relationship for mutual gain?

The Problem With Traditional Marketing

Judy Glicken needed people. Specifically, MORE people, at all hours of the day, to wander into her high-end bakery/café in downtown Weaverville, North Carolina. Her business was a classic example of what happens when you place quality product and service above everything else. The costs get out of control and the only thing that will push the business over the profit line is sales, sales and more sales.

When I entered the scene, daytime business was pretty good. The old Main Street corner building which housed the café had high ceilings and grand arched windows. Judy brought in a Feng Shui consultant early on and the result was what I consider the perfect little café. All we needed now was more people. Weekend evenings had been the worst, with only random passers-by stopping in for a piece of cake and some conversation. In her corner, Judy knew that she was the only bakery/café in town. At the other end of the rink was the greatest challenge of all—Weaverville's population of just 2,416.

We met over coffee and set forth a plan. Before I left, Judy pointed out that her advertising contract was up for renewal. I advised that she throw it in the garbage and commit those funds to a few strong non-profit organizations that would, in turn, support her. She agreed and I went back to the office to make some calls.

In less than a month, Saturday nights at the Well Bred Bakery Café were full of people and activity. Not only was the foot traffic great, but there were articles popping up in local newspapers about the café each month. In the more rural area to the north, residents of towns up to 20 miles away began to make regular appearances at the café. It took just about 2 months from the beginning of the marketing project for us to see natives of the nearby city of Asheville getting into their cars and taking the short road trip out to Weaverville to check out the café that everyone was talking about. What is amazing about this is not the fact that people got on the road to check out a local food trend. What is amazing about this is that the city of Asheville (est. population 68,889 in 2002) has over 25 independently owned cafes within 3 miles of its downtown center. Why were people journeying away from local cafes and bakeries just to visit a small town bakery? Because the bakery had succeeded in creating an endeared, supportive community that would drive for miles to enjoy the dynamic environment offered in the cafe. But the best part—Judy Glicken is, without a doubt one of our easiest clients on the books.

I told Judy to cancel her advertising, not because it wouldn't gain her business, but because for a fraction of her advertising budget, she would gain 800% or more business by engaging in a community-oriented marketing project. I'll be the first to call out, advertising does work and in some cases, it works very well. But the 300 year old advertising ecosystem, where organizations of all kinds subsidize media in exchange for the opportunity to make an impression on consumers, is breaking down at rapid speed. My highest advice is to put your money elsewhere.

The worst part about our current marketing system is that it is dominated by interruption-based solicitations. When a commercial comes over the airwaves or a billboard grabs your attention, it is an interruption. When a telemarketer calls or a popup window appears while you are browsing the internet, it is an interruption. Writes Steven Hayden of contemporary media campaigns: "You're soaking in it. Blasted, assaulted, insulted, surrounded, distracted, hypnotized and occasionally seduced every day." This is not to say that our weary populace will rise up against the institution and do away with advertising for good. Quite the contrary, advertising is here to stay. But for local and regional businesses—especially the emerging, socially responsible businesses that wish to grow—the next generation of marketers will tender poorer results per advertising dollar spent than any generation before. We'll talk more about advertising in Part 3 of this book. I'll introduce some excellent (and far more affordable) forms of media which DO tender results that very few businesses take advantage of.

There is much more to marketing than advertising. What's more, each traditional form has a counterpart in community-oriented marketing that is more effective, affordable and measurable in its result. It isn't that traditional marketing doesn't work. It can work very well. The problem which faces most marketers is that it usually does not bring in *enough* business to justify the expense. Other problems with traditional marketing and public relations include:

- Most direct mail gets thrown away.

- Most radio & TV commercials get muted or go ignored

- Most websites do not focus on generating business and cannot be found in the search engines

- Most newsletters are just plain boring

- Most print ads are not cost effective and often are placed in the wrong publications

- Most brochures are never read

- Most attempts to sponsor the nonprofit community are passive and never planned out for maximum results

- Most donations to nonprofits are never noticed

- Most marketing just plain costs too much

The good news is that transitioning your development model towards a community-oriented marketing approach will systematically provide answers to almost every problem listed here. And while a book like this one cannot teach you how to design a better printed piece, it can give you ideas and guidelines to take to the graphic design firm.

Why Community-Oriented Marketing Generates More Business And Quality Referrals Than Other Type Of Marketing

I began thinking about community-oriented marketing while I was working for an Internet Service Provider called Siteleader.com, which was headquartered in suburban Chicago, Illinois. One of the interesting things I immediately noticed upon assuming my post was that out of almost one million domain registration and web hosting customers, Siteleader had less than 200 customers that actually lived in the Chicago vicinity. Part of my job as Executive V.P. of Customer & Technical Support was to find out why customers were leaving and taking their business to competing companies. At the same time I was under pressure to increase customer referrals and generate sales. It was while researching our database and communicating with clients that I made a series of principle discoveries:

- 86% of customers who left and took their business to competing companies were the same customers who had been attracted in the first place to Siteleader by traditional forms of marketing. The competing companies usually got our customers to join them in exchange for a much cheaper monthly fee. (It is interesting to note that almost every single web hosting company that mass marketed our customers based on lower fees went out of business or restructured to higher fees within 2 years)

- Of those customers who were attracted by traditional marketing and later transferred their business elsewhere, only 7% ever passed a single referral to another friend or colleague during their time with Siteleader.

- On the other hand, 60% of all customers who were referred by friends or colleagues renewed their ISP services year after year (based on a 4 year study).

- Of those customers who were referred by friends or colleagues, 4 out of 5 of them, at some time or another, referred at least one *more* friend or colleague to Siteleader for hosting or domain registration services.

Here's the kicker. The average ISP customer whose services included the web hosting of a nonprofit organization referred 3-4 new customers each year, many of them finding their way to Siteleader by clicking on the link at the bottom of the referrer's web page. These customers were sent in by referrals from nonprofit organizations, so they are Values Partners. What's more, the small business customers whose businesses provided services to networked groups of people (catering companies, publishing companies, healthcare professionals, etc) referred almost as many customers—again, many of them finding their way to Siteleader by clicking on the link at the bottom of the page.

We already explained the common values dynamic which drives an easier and more sincere sale from the point of initial contact. We know that when the first point of contact between the company and the consumer is based on shared values, the sale is easier to make. When your business sells its service or product to a Values Partner, what is the likelihood that this customer is going to switch to a competitor when a salesman shows up at their door? Let's say you've got a dog named Spot. You have been paying Bob the dog walker for a month and little Spot adores him. You met Bob through one of your valued community channels and he follows the community-oriented sales approach we talked about earlier. Let's say that Barbara the dog walker sends you a piece of direct mail that offers a 30% cheaper price than Bob's. Do you call up Bob and cancel his service? No! You keep paying him 30% more because you've had a strong connection with him from the beginning. Barbara is just a tourist. She can't possibly stand up to Bob The Values Partner.

Some of the most exciting results of a community-oriented marketing project are the quality referrals and the potential for growth through word of mouth. When you grow your business through community-oriented marketing, the first three to six months typically generate as much new business as traditional marketing. Then comes the snowball. Provided you back up your commitment to the community with a commitment to delivering a quality product or service, your incoming business that's generated by referrals will grow like nothing you have ever experienced before. I get calls every week from clients who are ecstatic about this. They just can't believe how much business one can generate from referrals.

What I'm talking about is old school to big business. Earthlink spent millions of dollars establishing a referral program that rewarded referrals by granting free service to the referrer. Many businesses, after closing a sale, ask customers for the names and phone numbers of friends who might also be interested in their service or product. These days it's commonplace. Long distance companies, cell phone companies, gyms and even private schools encourage referrals by offering a reward. But rewarding referrals is on the low end of what is possible. Do you remember earlier, when we talked about creating a compelling and memorable experience? The degree to which you do this, combined with the tenacity by which you focus on community empowerment, is the equation which will compel more referrals than any rewards program ever devised.

When I was the CEO at New Human, Inc., one of my favorite clients of all time was Alan Brown. Alan Brown is the President of Anthony Robbins & Associates, Inc, a business which puts on personal growth seminars using the Anthony Robbins method of experiential teaching. My company built his a simple web page with a shopping cart for audio products and books. About a month later, I decided to attend one of his seminars. A few hours into the seminar, while he was presenting on stage, Alan announced to the audience that I ran the greatest, most professional web design company in all of Chicago. He had me stand up and everyone cheered for me. He then went on to spend about 5 minutes telling the group, in detail, about what a great experience he had had with my company and encouraged them to call me if they needed web design work. Because 7 out of 10 people at any personal growth seminar are business owners or executives, I gained tens of thousands of dollars from one single referral. And guess what…. I originally met Alan Brown through a nonprofit activity he participates in each year, wherein thousands of baskets of food are delivered to struggling families during the Thanksgiving Holiday.

Malcolm Gladwell wrote an excellent book called *The Tipping Point*, wherein he produced piles of research on the phenomena of "word of mouth epidemics." He opens the book with the story of how the shoe brand, Hush Puppies, made a multimillion dollar comeback after falling into obscurity and facing extinction. The best part of the Hush Puppies comeback is that their parent corporation never spent a dime on marketing. To summarize the story, a few popular people in New York's club scene started wearing vintage Hush Puppies to the clubs as a fashion statement. Envious club goers hit the vintage clothing stores and cleaned out the entire 2nd hand circuit in New York of Hush Puppy shoes. Then the fashion designers began to incorporate the trend into their emerging lines. Suddenly the retailers who, despite the brand's decline, had continued to carry Hush Puppies, could not keep them on their shelves. The trend spread coast to coast and the brand never spent a dollar on marketing to make it happen. That kind of business growth is a fantasy for so many business owners, yet it is entirely possible.

Do you know who James Redfield is? Have you ever heard of his novel, *The Celestine Prophecy*? James Redfield's 1993 novel is probably the greatest of all self-published novel success stories. According to Publishing Trends, *The Celestine Prophecy* was the #1 international bestseller of 1996 (#2 in 1995). In 1995 and 1996, it was the #1 American book in the world. This amazing novel spent almost 4 years on the "New York Times" bestseller list and also appeared on bestseller lists across the globe. After just 6 months, the novel had over 100,000 copies in print, was in all 50 states, and was appearing in countries around the world. How did he do it? James Redfield did nothing but write an outstanding novel which provided the reader with a memorable, enlightening and compelling experience. The success of the book was attributed purely to it being passed from one individual to another. What Redfield's book achieved was a shocking sales boom, spread in epidemic proportions by word of mouth. After the self-published book was brought to the attention of Warner Books, the media giant bought the rights for $800,000 and published the hard cover edition in March, 1994. It remained on the bestseller list for more than three years.

Applying Good Karma To Business—From The Inside Out

"Civic connections help make us healthy, wealthy and wise," writes Robert Putnam in *Bowling Alone*, a book which explores the history of civic life in America throughout the past three decades. Sociological research teaches us that cities which are rich with interactive, interconnected communities have less crime, higher standards of health and a higher quality of life than cities that are comprised of isolated individuals.

While section two will focus on the practical applications of a community-oriented marketing model, much of the stories and ideas we are exploring now are about encouraging a shift in our *thinking* models. Community-oriented marketing isn't just a plan. It's much more than a series of actions which propel you towards your goal. It is a way of doing business that extends into the way in which we all experience the world.

So I ask of you to consider. What would happen if just 100 businesses in your city all began to market themselves using a community-oriented approach? If each business spends just $250 per month supporting community organizations, at the end of the year we would fine an extra $300,000 being funneled into a brighter future for everyone.

Most businesses, even small businesses spend much more than $250 per month on marketing. There is room to make an investment in the future. The resources are there. It's the way in which you, as a professional, see and use those resources, which will make the difference. So, in the light of all that we have explored so far, my hope is that you are inspired to try on this new way of thinking—in business and in life. My greatest hope: that you resolve to join an elite community of enlightened businesses who put the law of attraction to work for them and in doing so, apply good karma to their businesses from the inside out.

"Community Involvement is nothing new to The Body Shop—it is a concept that has always been an integral part of our business and is vital to us going forward into the 21st century. As a socially responsible business we campaign for the protection of the environment, human and civil rights and against animal testing within the cosmetics and toiletries industry.

Volunteering supports this work enabling us to positively contribute to the local, national and global communities in which we operate. We are proud of our employees' enthusiastic involvement in their local communities and actively encourage their participation at the same time as considering the changing expectations of society and the growing environmental and ethical concerns. In understanding this we realize that our support is fundamental and continually explore imaginative new ways of working."

—The Body Shop

PART III

Community-Oriented Marketing In Action

Don't Move A Muscle—There Is A Bomb Under Your Chair

11 QUESTIONS THAT WILL MAKE OR BREAK YOUR BUSINESS

At this point, you probably have some ideas and are eager to get started. So far, we have been considering the ideology behind community-oriented marketing. I shared some examples and gave some general advice. In this section, we get down to business. But before you initiate any marketing project, it is necessary that you ask yourself some specific questions about what you want to accomplish.

I speak from personal experience when I caution that dashing into a marketing project without taking this section seriously is risky. It would be like walking onto a stage in a designer tuxedo and putting on a fantastic presentation, only to realize halfway through that your fly is unzipped. I beg you! Do not engage in community-oriented marketing until you have explored each of the following questions. In almost every marketing effort I have seen fail, the missing link was due to one of the following questions going unanswered.

1. Are you personally capable of attracting and creating abundance?

The single most damaging *and likely* threat to any marketing project is the mental attitude and focus of the individuals doing the marketing. Negative expectations, self-limited thinking, unwillingness to accept responsibility and a lack of self confidence are the main killers of any marketing project. Having a "positive attitude" on the outside is not enough to counteract *what is transpiring on the inside* if you are not yet ready to start marketing your product.

Here again, I am speaking of the Law of Attraction. Believe me when I tell you that it works *both* ways! Whatever you put out—positive or negative, cynically self-serving or sincerely generous, self-defeating or high flying—will come back to you like the Ghost of Christmas Past. Whatever you expect is *exactly* what you will get.

If the Law of Attraction applies to everyone, you may be wondering why so many good, honest, sincere business owners close their doors every day. Why do the nicest people who run the most generous and community-oriented business in the world end up bankrupt despite all of their efforts? Even churches and homeless shelters are forced to go under every week in America. Why? Because the Law of Attraction must be actively and consciously applied.

A great example of how the Law of Attraction can work AGAINST your business lies in cash-crunch sales. When businesses are in financial trouble, extra pressure is put on their salespeople. In the case of many small business entrepreneurs, all of the pressure falls onto the shoulders of one individual. When this happens, despite the highest values and intentions, a cloud falls over the actions and behavior of everyone involved. Most of us have experienced periods in our lives when finances ran thin and economic survival was at the forefront of our minds. Stress and perpetual concern about money can cast a shadow over our lives. That shadow affects business life particularly because suddenly each sale becomes extremely important. Think about attraction. Like attracts like. If you are concerned about money every day, you will primarily attract clients with little or none to spend. This formula applies to every aspect of human personality. Dishonest businesses attract dishonest customers. Worrisome businesses attract worrisome customers. Disorganized businesses attract chaotic circumstances.

The Sensible City used to work with a company that provided decorations to interior designers. The proprietor of the business was a fine artist who was weary of working in homes and wanted us to help him attract corporate contracts. I'll call him John. I liked John because he was good at smiling. After a few conversations, I could tell he had a fantastic understanding of business and I was impressed by his organizational skills. Through my own networking channels, I was able to set up an introduction for him at a fine hotel in downtown Chicago that was remodeling. Both the hotel Marketing Director and Interior Designer saw his work and were excited about hiring him to work on their renovation project. 2 weeks later, I asked my client how things were going with the hotel. "*Horrible*," he replied. "They don't want to spend any money and their designer wants to run the show." In the interest of saving the deal, I contacted the hotel Marketing Director. Her reply was: "We really liked his work, told him our budget per-room and asked for a proposal. I haven't heard back." When I asked John why he hadn't proposed, he complained that their budget of $250 per room was not enough for him. "It would barely cover my costs."

My advice to John from the beginning of the deal had been to get into that hotel by any means necessary. Why should John have negotiated a deal with the hotel? Because he had no business clients and so long as he wasn't losing any money, a luxury hotel (which is frequently used by corporate travelers) is a foot in the door of multiple corporate ecosystems. If he were to have simply focused on delivering high quality prints instead of oil paintings for the walls, he could have parlayed a nice profit from the job, not to mention networking and referrals. When I posed this solution, he replied that he didn't have any wholesale framing relationships to make it financially possible. Rather than counsel him on taking initiative and locating a framing situation that would work, I let the issue drop. Although we continued to assist John in his marketing, we eventually had to close the file because with each opportunity placed before his company, something was always wrong. When planning projects, he would often say "I can't see how that is going to work." Sure enough, when things did not work, he would let us know.

This may seem like an extreme example, but marketing consultants reading this book will agree that this and other personality challenges are commonplace obstructions to growth. In Jeffrey A. Timmon's study of entrepreneurial characteristics (*New Venture Creation: A Guide To Small Business Development*), he shares his findings that successful entrepreneurs are disappointed by failure, but not discouraged by it. He further explores the ways in which successful professionals use failure as learning experiences in order to avoid further problems and mistakes popping up. John isn't a bad guy by any measure, but he, like many business owners, is the main obstacle on his path to prosperity.

On the other hand, I meet professionals every day that amaze me because their attitude is the only thing they have going for them. I know business owners who, despite having lousy marketing pieces and a complete lack of knowledge for sales, surpass all of their competition through attitude alone. I call it "Playing Full-Out." In sports, playing full-out means tapping into your highest potential. Marketers who are always looking for ways to make the most of a situation and get the best return on their investment in time, money or effort always tender better results.

I will revisit this aspect throughout the book. There always is a wrong way to do the right thing. That is why working out your own limitations (we all have them) is the best way to begin a marketing project. There are many books and audio programs which address this subject. To help choose the right program for you, I encourage you to work with a professional coach on these matters. On our website at www.community-oriented.com, along with a list of great books on all topics discussed in this one, I have a directory of coaching organizations in North America and The United Kingdom whom you can contact directly.

2. Who is your target market and where can you find them receptive to your message?

This sounds like a boring, general marketing question to many people. But 9 out of every 10 businesses I encounter have a poor or deficient definition of their target market. In most cases, businesses find one or two demographical categories to chase after, but neglect to explore the rest of their community. The questions below will help you describe your future customer in terms of who they are, where they live, what they do for a living and what their needs are. You'll use the answers to these questions later as you get busy marketing yourself, so write down your responses:

- What is the household income range of your ideal customer? If your customer base spans several income classes, list each one.
- Do they spend or do they save? If they spend, where do they dispose of their income?
- Are they conservative? Liberal? Religious? Spiritual? Seeking answers?
- Where do they live? Do they rent or own real estate?
- Do they have children? Are they active in family living?
- Are they environmentally responsible? Outdoors-oriented?
- Are they male? Female? How old are they? Are they health-conscious?
- Where do they go/what do they do for entertainment?
- Are they happy or sad? Self-actualizing or frustrated? Socially content or lonely?
- What do they wear? What kind of car do they drive? Where do they shop?
- Do they travel? Where do they go?

My business questionnaire has over 100 questions like the ones above. Sometimes people get confused when I ask these questions of them, but if you follow the model of community-oriented selling we talked about before, this information comes in handy for The Encore. You'll find that picking apart your best customers is ideal for building relationships and generating sales. The more focused you are, the more likely you are to experience returns on your marketing efforts.

3. *What do you want to accomplish?*

- Generate inquiries? For what?

- Get someone to try a free or discounted consultation?

- Get someone to request information?

- To brand your product? To improve your reputation? To create awareness? To provide information?

- To announce something (a new service, an appearance, a result)?

This question is especially important for identity pieces. Most brochures, pamphlets, cards, websites and mailings are for "general marketing." While this approach can generate business, a FOCUSED approach will generate 4 times the response. For example, my chiropractor's website (www.cafeoflifeasheville.com) in Asheville, NC has the specific focus of generating awareness and providing information. Because of this, you'll find a website geared towards information and "Meeting the Doc." On the other hand, my associate Tom Heck's website (www.teachmeteamwork.com) has the specific focus of getting people to sign up for a highly useful community portal that is packed with multimedia tools and resources for educators and coaches.

If you have more than one focus, address each one carefully. For example, Jane Goodall's organization (www.janegoodall.org) focuses first on distributing information and second on generating donations and community support. The Sensible City (www.community-oriented.com) also focuses first on distributing information, second on generating business and third on fostering a web community of its own.

4. *What is your position on the market growth scale?*

If you are like me, you need a strong cup of coffee and a sense of humor to keep up with daily business news. Not to mention a weekly massage therapist and yoga classes. Yes, yes, the business world is changing. The economy is strong, the economy is weak, the economy is strong again. Naughty executives, terrorists and hackers want to raid our capitalist afternoon picnic. Now, as I write this, spending is up again. Tomorrow it could all collapse again, so we'll stick to the lay-offs and slash the catered lunches.

Economic growth and decline are typically times in which major market segments are passing through the major phases of market growth. Whatever your business project, you fall into one of the following categories of market maturation:

1. Market Introduction Phase: The "innovation" stage of a market is the most exciting time to be involved. This is when fresh information, products and technology are introduced to society. In this phase, the product's future is determined by whether or not it is commercially accepted.

2. Growth and Distribution Phase: When I pioneered an internet business in 1997, it was successful not because I was a great internet architect, but because in 1997, the dotcom trend was in its Growth and Distribution Phase. During this phase, the average business person can make a decent living, a spirited entrepreneur can get rich and the corporate systems can achieve shocking financial growth.

3. Maturity and Commoditization Phase: In this phase, entrepreneurs often (though not always) run for cover while larger businesses make cut-backs and sustain themselves at slower rates of growth. This is a phase responsible for much of America's failing small businesses. Professionals see that a lot of money has been made and chase after the tails of the Market Growth and Distribution Phase. This is a phase dominated by fierce price-point competition and limited opportunities for growth.

4. Sustained Service Demand Phase: This phase applies primarily to services-oriented businesses that offer essential support to the entire business panorama or to markets which have survived The Maturity and Commoditization Phase. This can also apply to businesses which will always be in-demand by the general public. A few examples include attorneys, certified public accountants, mechanics, and cleaning companies. Keep in mind, however, that with each of these professions, the first 3 phases often apply and are usually based on the evolution of competition in local markets.

It is very important that you accurately assess your position on the growth chart. For each phase of market growth, there are several strata of support opportunities to be had. The key to long term survival for any company is in understanding the day-to-day progress of the market. With this knowledge, business decisions can be proactive rather than reactive. For example, during the Growth and Distribution Phase of the dotcom boom, office supply companies, telecommunications companies and a host of other business development companies made huge profits by simply providing services to the internet businesses that were taking off. Similarly and ironically, office liquidation firms and corporations with the financial strength to make acquisitions gained tremendously as the Maturity and Commoditization Phase of the dotcom boom took to the stage. Companies like Andover Consulting Group (www.andovercg.com) leveraged the resources of ebay.com (a company that survived the dotcom bust by delivering an outstanding, useful way for thousands of entrepreneurs to create incomes in a declining economy) to liquidate the technological resources of companies across America.

5. What do you offer that sets you completely apart?

So what do you offer that cannot be found anywhere else in your city? What puts you at the very top of the pyramid? Far too many businesses would answer: "Better product/service for a reasonable price." That combination is a recipe for commoditization and slow growth.

Here, though, is an example of a business that separated itself. The Fredericksburg Herb Farm (www.fredericksburgherbfarm.com) in Fredericksburg, Texas is located over an hour's drive away from either San Antonio or Austin in a small antiques town setting. They are not on the main road. The economy has hit this area with a depressing decline in tourism sales. But whenever I visit my grandmother in San Antonio, I insist that we make the trip. The owners set themselves apart and poised themselves for long term growth by adding value in every direction and by transforming an herb farm into a memorable, compelling experience. They have a day spa, a bed and breakfast, a wonderful gourmet restaurant, 3 different creative and fun gift shops, a walking course where you can learn about herbs, a bunny farm, a cookbook, an annual Herbfest and a forum by which the community and visiting tourists can attend classes, lectures and workshops on everything from gardening to personal health.

There are many ways to set yourself apart and you don't always have to go to so much work. In a city fierce with competition, Mark and Nancy Tarlowe (a chiropractor and a yoga teacher) opened up a combined wellness center (www.awakening-heart.com), immediately creating an advantage which set themselves apart from the many yoga and chiropractic settings in Asheville. Heather Pike of Pike Works Design Studios (www.pikeworks.com) has a reputation in Memphis, TN for being a woman who can find anything and create a themed space or event that is exactly what her clients want. Merely being the only professional in your field who can act as a "bird dog" often makes all of the difference in the world. When mid-south executives need a themed event and don't know who to call, they call Heather Pike.

Setting yourself apart is more than a way of leveling the playing ground with your competition. It is also about creating a unique approach that will broadcast the authenticity of your socially responsible principles. On all of these fronts, without your own powerful voice and character, your marketing efforts will fade into the backdrop of your competitor's efforts.

6. What are the features of what you are offering? What does it look like? Where is it? When is it?

Please be specific. This is especially important for print advertising.

- Is it animal, vegetable or mineral?

- Is it a service or a product?

- What benefits are you offering?

- Does it make the world a better place?

- What specific problems does it solve for the individual, the community or the world? What opportunities does it create or help to exploit?

- Does it make or save them money? Save time?

- Does it feel good? Taste good? Sound good?

- Does it make their job, family or private life easier?

An unfortunate ripple effect of the creative ad wars that took place throughout the 1990's is the lingering genre of vague ads which focus on shock value. You see them every day, whether you take notice or not. The burst of the dotcom bubble was mainly to blame, with families of ads which would portray an image, a compelling word or series of words and a URL (web address). Of course, the intention of large companies was to brand their names. But what often happens is that small business owners model the ads of more successful companies and hope to receive dramatic results. Which brings us to the next question:

7. Are you Branding? Marketing? Publicizing?

I am going to define a few terms in my own words and you can make the distinctions.

- Marketing: Reach out, grab your audience and attract them to your business with the goal of building sales.

- Branding: Clearly define your image or product's image by associating it with the emotional needs and practical demands of the public. Then get that image or product's image out into the public eye through the consistent delivery of that image over a period of time. When your brand becomes stagnant or loses prominence in the face of competition, repeat the process.

- Public Relations: This is one of the most misunderstood terms in the business world. I could easily offer a dozen definitions. But in the application of community-oriented marketing, PR *is* community-oriented marketing. It is about your relationship with the community. It should be noted that public relations, when drawing up a budget, is typically the most intangible marketing effort in terms of return on investment.

I ask this question because even I, after years of experience, still forget to get clear about this from time to time. But it is very important when making spending decisions. Simply ask yourself: What is my outcome and is it worth the expense?

8. Why should your prospect respond right away? What will happen if they do or don't?

Coupons expire for a reason. The word "buy" is more often than not followed by "now" in many stores. Chains offer 10% off of the customer's first purchase if they "sign up now." 50% off between 2 and 3 PM. Must be redeemed within 10 days. Hurry in before it's too late. The first 100 customers will receive a special bonus. Refer a friend before May 15th and save an additional $100. You get the idea. This question is simple, but equally important. Unless you have a fortune to spend on marketing, your marketing efforts should encourage an immediate introduction.

9. Are you ready for them when they come?

Please don't start marketing yourself until you have every single identity piece completed. If you have a website (which you absolutely should), make sure that it is not "under construction" when your marketing piece hits the streets. If you operate a small business, make sure that your answering system isn't a $10 machine you bought on sale. If you say that your hours are from 9-5, get there at 8:30. This question is mainly focused on new business startups or revamps, but you should all get the point. Whether you are or not, you must at least *look* like the best choice in town when your audience arrives.

10. Are you willing to accept responsibility for failure and if so, how much money can you afford to lose?

You may have picked up this book because it offers "sure-fire tactics" to creating results. Every marketing book I have ever read talks about "making sure" you get a return on investment. Most authors selling a marketing system or a consulting practice will boast how if you follow the right process, you *cannot fail*. But in reality, the likelihood is that not everything you are going to do will work. In fact, for most businesses, 15-30% of all marketing efforts tender almost no results at all. In my own professional experience, I have worked with many clients who simply could not fail in any of our marketing projects, and yet they did.

Why can't we guarantee the big bucks? Because every business is different and approaches the market with assets and liabilities unique to its particular communications strategy. The job of a marketer is to deliver an attentive audience. The rest is up to the business itself. I was talking with my friend Jerry in Los Angeles the other day about an ad that he ran in the local paper. He was complaining about the paper itself and how "that newspaper tendered no results at all." He was even considering calling the paper and demanding his money back (which, by the way, is a near impossibility to accomplish).

Jerry's business was a retail office supplies and do-it-yourself copy shop. I quietly and respectfully offered a question: "Is it possible that the burden of failure lies with the ad itself?"

"Absolutely not," he said. "I paid a designer 350 bucks to lay it out professionally. My designer is one of the best guys in town."

I asked him to email me a copy of the ad so that I could take a look for myself. Within 5 seconds of viewing it, I could see why the ad tendered no results. My friend's designer had created a beautiful, high-impact ad. It certainly jumped off the page. But it failed to give the reader a good reason to come in or call. There was no discount or new service being offered. The ad basically consisted of a logo and a summarized description of services, along with the words "Now Open."

The moral of this story is three-fold:

- You must be prepared for 15-30% of all of your marketing efforts to fail.
- When they do fail, you must find out why and use the information constructively.

- Once you have used this failure as a building block for future marketing projects, you must redefine it as "education" rather than "failure."

After going over this approach with my friend, I asked him how he was going to share the results of his ad with his business partner. He replied: "Educational!" And while many readers won't look forward to the first moral of this story, anyone who has been in business for a while will likely nod in agreement. My hope is that with this awareness, you will be less likely to go barreling into a marketing project without asking yourself these questions first.

11. How will you measure the success of this marketing effort? How many? What kind? How soon? How much?

These are simple questions, based primarily on profit and loss. Their deeper implications lie in choosing the right marketing activity by researching its likely results. If you have a retail business, your marketing should focus on creating an increase in measurable foot traffic and sales. If you are a real estate agent, you should be able to measure your results by the number of introductions to potential buyers. If you sell widgets online or over the phone, your success will most likely be measured by your actual sales.

The equation then becomes simple. If you want lots of foot traffic, market yourself to a large number of people. If you want a small number of large sales, market yourself to a focused group of interested buyers with buying power. If you want a rapid response, market yourself to an active, responsive audience.

12. Do you need the dog and pony show?

It was his nose that brought Emil Anishanslin to the Rio Grande Valley. In the 1940's, the Valley was wide open for commercial development and when he first arrived with a group of potential investors, the smell of orange groves in bloom and mesquite in the air were all that he needed to make the decision to move. A few years later, business was booming. Emil sold real estate by day and insurance by night. Before long, he was only selling real estate. He retired early, financially independent and satisfied. His experience as an entrepreneur is, by my standards the American Dream. Here's why:

Mr. Anishanslin was my grandfather. When my grandmother told me the story of their move to The Rio Grande Valley, she was quick to show me this photo. "People figured that since we didn't have to pay all that money for a fancy office, maybe they would get a better deal when buying from us." After the war, Emil was amongst a minority of real estate brokers willing to process "Right To Buy" loans—a government program for GI's returning home which involved heavy paperwork and tendered lower profits for real estate professionals. Choosing to follow a profit-by-volume business approach, he welcomed returning soldiers and built his wealth by giving them the same level of respect that he would treat a more profitable buyer. So before you spend 2 years of profits building out the ultimate space in which to do business—ask yourself: "Is this a necessary step for creating an ideal experience for my customer?"

19 Community-Oriented Marketing Techniques You Can Take To The Bank

Now comes my favorite part—the guts of community-oriented marketing. This is where I hope you will sit up in your chair, grab a pen and start taking notes. Community-oriented marketing, as I mentioned earlier, is a holistic and systemized approach. It is possible that a single action listed in this section will take you where you want to go. But in most cases, it is through the application of as many of these methods as possible, implemented over an extended period of time, that will engender the best results.

The idea is to use this section as a starting point for developing your own creative marketing activities. There are hundreds of effective techniques that are available in community-oriented marketing, so do yourself a favor. Check out *1001 Ways To Market Your Services*, by Rick Crandall and *Off-The-Wall Marketing Ideas*, by Michaels & Karpoqicz. These books, although highly mainstream, both offer quite a few ideas that fall right in line with the community-oriented approach.

To follow are some of the most frequently used approaches which consistently get results. They are not listed in any particular order of importance and many of them are nothing new to savvy marketers. When I talk about getting involved with nonprofits, for example, this has been going on for hundreds of years. But read closely. There is always an opportunity to improve upon anything that is old. The key to community-oriented marketing is that you integrate the old, while staying on the lookout for opportunities to make a values-based introduction.

1. Community-Oriented Advertising

Tim Dyrkacz, a Chicago C.P.A. who was in my networking group, had no idea what he was getting into when he purchased a simple $85 advertising space in a playbill for a local professional dance company. Only 3 months after the curtain fell, he reported back to me that he had made over a thousand dollars out of that one $85 ad through a total of three calls he had received from it. A few months later, I spoke with George Steinburg, a mortgage broker who had taken out a full page ad for $265. George had turned up nothing. If you read the play-bill, you would see that George's ad was larger and nicer than Tim's. So why is it that Tim ended up getting results?

I wanted to know the answer, so I spent about half an hour on the phone with Tim, George and the marketing liaison for the dance company. In the end, Tim played full-out. After reserving the ad, he called the artistic director of the company to let her know that he supported her work and looked forward to the show. He then *designed an ad specifically for the audience*. His ad promoted himself as a creative entrepreneur who understands creative business finance. At the bottom of the ad, he gave congratulations to "all of the hard working dancers and professionals" who had come together to make the evening possible. George, on the other hand, hired a graphic designer to lay out his photograph, logo and marketing text onto a pleasing background. I have changed the names so that I don't offend or embarrass George in this example, but please read the point. Getting a return on investment from advertising is about:

- Speaking directly to the audience. Ask yourself what you can do to get their attention and win their hearts

- Going beyond just placing an ad. Find out what you can do to give support. Remember that whenever you buy advertising in a community organization, you are supporting them financially and making their work possible. Take advantage of this and remember that you are a hero in the community!

Here are some good ideas for community-oriented advertising. Again, you must contact these organizations and find out who their reader base is.

NEIGHBORHOOD NEWSPAPERS

Many neighborhoods have their own newspaper or newsletter. Your chamber of commerce can usually produce a demographical report of the residential population in that area. The advertising dollars you provide for these publications usually provides much-needed funds for the neighborhood association. Watch out for poorly distributed neighborhood media. Only advertise in neighborhoods with loyal readership. If you are unclear about this, ask how they are distributed. If they are only piled up at the community center, don't bite. On the other hand, some neighborhood newspapers are hand-delivered to every door in the district.

LOCAL ASSOCIATION, CIVIC GROUP AND BUSINESS CLIENT NEWSLETTERS/ COMMUNICATIONS

Many businesses send out a monthly or even quarterly newsletter to their customer base. Depending on how well you know the business providing this value-added service for their customers, you may be able to cross promote at no cost. Make sure the publication is well read by your target market. For example, I know a financial planner who advertised his services in his cosmetic surgeon's patient newsletter. There are many creative ways to advertise using this approach. The Sensible City often sends out advertisements and coupons for fellow business associates in our monthly invoices. This grassroots approach works well with many service-oriented businesses.

For example, you may want to appeal to vegetarians. Find out what groups there are out there which promote healthy living and ask if they have a periodical they send out. If you want to advertise to families, find the newsletters for after-school sports organizations and extra-curricular activities communities.

PLAYBILL ADVERTISING

This is the single most effective form of community-oriented advertising I have ever encountered. Music. Symphony. Dance. Theatre. Opera. Think about it. What is the likelihood that your advertisement will be noticed? Read? Even scrutinized? Every time I have ever been to a concert or performing arts production, I see hoards of people reading those playbills. The ones who stay seated during intermission are the best but what really amazes me is how many people actually take the playbill with them when they leave the show.

NICHE NEWSPAPERS

I admit that I am a huge fan of independent media. Most cities in North America are now producing a weekly newspaper that focuses on well-written literary content and covers local events, happenings, politics and community issues not covered by mainstream newspapers. The only challenge with these papers is that they typically have so much advertising and have such a broad reader base that it is difficult for me to justify their expense. So here is a test that you can try at home. Create an ad that focuses on generating business and run it for 3-6 months. In order to gauge effectiveness offer a discount or coupon that customers must redeem. If after six months you haven't gotten any solid results, give it up and stick to the smaller publications.

Other niche newspapers which have proven more effective are newspapers which focus on local business, outdoor enthusiasts, the legal community, the gay & lesbian community, religious/spiritual audiences, women in business, environmental issues and more.

My old internet business used to get leads from an advertisement I would run in Chicago's pet community newspaper of all things. Earlier in this book, we talked about getting out and getting to know your city. Locating these advertising opportunities is an easy side-job while you are strolling around. As I said before, advertising is *everywhere*. Your job is to find out ways in which you can advertise while simultaneously making a values-based introduction.

2. Start A Radio Show

When Coburn Gardner asked me to help him market his business, I wasn't sure exactly where to start. Coburn is a professional psychic. Not the kind of psychic that conjures stereotypical images of a gypsy dressed in bright colors, but a simple man with a "down home" appearance who just happens to be able to foresee the future. Coburn's long-range vision is to teach people that "being psychic" is really just about listening to your own intuition and trusting the information it feeds you.

Again, because I love a challenge, The Sensible City took Coburn on as a client. I won't explore the many things that we did which gained him exposure and business, but I will point out one of the most successful items on the agenda: to create a local call-in radio show. I won't take full credit for it. Coburn did most of the grunt work. But here's how it works:

1. Design a show that will generate active listeners. Find out what the community needs and fill that void by creating a radio show that delivers an emotional, compelling and memorable experience for the listener. By "creating a show" I mean type up a proposal in a professional, organized format. If you have the funds, consider renting a recording studio and sound engineer to create a mock-up of your proposed show. Be creative. Look for ways to move away from the standard call-in format and consider exciting interviews with community players instead.

2. Once you have designed the perfect talk radio show, start calling everyone you know in business and line up a few potential advertisers that will help fund the show. Radio stations create programming based on supporting ads. Delivering them a one-hour program in a box with sponsors that are ready to get started will guarantee you a serious consideration from most talk and public radio stations.

3. Approach each radio station in person with your proposal, but don't pressure them. Contact an ad sales representative and tell them that you have several advertising placements lined up (that will get their attention) and ask them who you should talk to in order to present your show. Give three copies of your proposal and call back in 3 business days if you have not heard a response. Follow up with the programming director and the sales director until you have a specific answer. If you don't get the show on the air, move on to the next radio station.

Starting a radio show is not necessarily easy and running a show can be overwhelming and stressful. It is a serious commitment that will take many hours out of every week. Don't create a show just to get business. If this is your goal, the listening community will be annoyed and your radio show will fail. Create instead a high-impact resource which fulfills a community's needs and let the business come in on its own.

3. Offer A Class, Workshop or Seminar

I met my former business partner, Jeremiah Desmarais, because he had the insight to create not just a class which he offered to the public, but an entire series of workshops, in which he inspired would-be entrepreneurs to take a leap and start their own businesses. But the subject of presenting to the public in order to grow your business is a difficult one for many marketers to take on because of the intention behind their activities as an "educator." Taking on this role does require a definite shift in perspective. Your job as a hero in the community is not to gather people into a room and direct them towards a sale. Your job is to find out what the public is in need of and to determine for which topic your expertise offers the greatest amount of useful information.

I ask that when you explore this option, you separate yourself from a sales-minded approach. Teach to empower. Educate to inspire. Uplift your target market community with information that will change their lives for the better. Afterwards, you can use the wrap-up at the end of your presentation to provide information about yourself and what you do. Leave the self-promotion for the last and keep it simple—just the facts.

Simply remember to deliver that emotionally empowering experience that your audience will never forget. You won't need to sell yourself. The experience you are giving away will reflect back on you and create the interest. Once you have delivered an educating and rewarding experience, move forward with the model we previously explored to generate community-oriented sales.

Finally, when planning your talk, class, lecture, workshop or seminar, aim big. It's always nice to put on a talk for ten people, but what about 50? 100? 300? What organizations or clubs would love to have you as a guest speaker? If you are presenting to your client base, ask that they bring a friend, family member or colleague with them to your talk. Whatever you do, don't just send out a press release and expect a crowd. Later, we will look at networking and how it may be your best bet for attracting an audience each time you speak in public.

4. Give It Away

I get calls on a regular basis from people who want to "pick my brain." Usually, I find that this is a nice way of asking for a "free consultation." My attorney complains about this all of the time, but I take it as an opportunity and as a compliment. In Brian Tracy's *Psychology of Achievement*, he repeats throughout the program that the best way to move forward quickly in business is to give twice as much as you expect to receive. The community-oriented approach to giving is to give often, give realistically (don't over-commit yourself) and give *strategically*. I know a smart consultant who walked into his area chamber of commerce and offered thousands of dollars of consulting services as a "patriotic contribution" to that chamber. The project was a redevelopment of their outdated, inefficient newsletter. The final product was a local business journal, produced by the chamber of commerce. This kind of contribution is staggering, even by my standards. But the result was a dramatic increase in member retention, as well as in advertising sales, which meant huge publicity for the chamber. Just six months later, funds were allocated to take it to "the next level" by building an online accompaniment, generating over $25,000 in actual income for the consultant.

Not long ago I read about an electronics retail store in Seattle that advertised that their stereos were on sale for "250 bananas." The term bananas was meant as a slang term for dollars, but a few consumers took the advertising literally and brought cases of bananas into the store. Because they didn't want to be accused of false advertising, they put the promotion to work for them by accepting the bananas and then donating them to the Seattle Zoo. Of course, they got a ton of publicity and it cost them very little.

What are some ways that you can give your product or service away with the strategic focus of potentially creating more business? NOTE: Not all of your efforts will result in immediate business. When planning gifts of time and effort, remember to detach yourself from a sales approach and give your all. Don't ruin your efforts by turning sour when the action doesn't achieve the results you intended. After all, the golden rule of giving is to give freely and without expectation of anything in return.

5. Print T-shirts and give them away

Do you ever think about how odd it is that across the planet, people spend their hard-earned dollars to advertise for corporations? In America, you cannot walk down a crowded city street in the summer time without being marketed by the garments of passers by. In most cases, these "marketers" actually paid to display the brand on their shirts! I remember when I was in college at The University of Memphis, I passed a table in the administration building on registration day and immediately stopped, turned around, and went back to the table to sign up for a credit card I didn't want. Why? Because the credit card company was offering not one, not two, but *three* free t-shirts to anyone who would apply. And since I hadn't done laundry in weeks, this was an offer I couldn't refuse.

I encourage give-aways. They have a nice way of giving back to you. They're a great example of the circular process that makes the community-oriented approach an honest-to-goodness practical marketing tool. I know a suburban gym owner in San Francisco who "rewards" his long-term members with a shirt that says, "Ask me how I got this great body" across the back, with his logo on the front. What are some ways you can transform the public into a walking advertisement?

6. Entertain Them

Last year, how many social events did you attend? There are always opportunities to entertain your community. In local news publications, the entertainment pages are typically amongst the most well-read sections. Alan Moore of AMI Consulting Group is well known for his "donor parties." These are invitation-only "appreciation dinners" for the individuals and businesses who have contributed to select non-profit groups in which he is involved. Other businesses focus on smaller events with greater frequency. If you have a retail space that you want to attract the community into, bring in music and other festivities that will engage and entertain your shoppers. If your business is more service-oriented, put on events or heavily engage yourself in other events which draw your market.

The Well-Bred Bakery has made a science of entertaining the public. Our community-oriented marketing project for them consisted primarily of entertainment activities promoted with supporting media releases. When you ask the public to patronize your food-selling establishment, you are inviting them in for an experience. If the food quality is poor, they won't return. Yet even the highest standards in food quality and preparation will do you no good if your ambience is lousy. Going out, after all, to a specialty eatery is more than getting a bite to eat. Eating in these circumstances is also a social event. Through live entertainment we infused the café with a spirited atmosphere and a vitalizing feel—perfect for social conviviality.

Our project, however, addressed more than ambience. The Well-Bred Bakery used entertainment as a media tool, as well. Because the focus was not only to increase night-time traffic, but also to draw in the neighboring Asheville population, we only booked Asheville bands for the first few months. We focused on well-connected, well-supported bands that were willing to come out and play for tips. This strategy created a lively ambience, drew in the hometown populace, brought in the nearby Asheville crowd, who are avid supporters of their musicians, and produced great media coverage. Wow! What more could you ask of a marketing strategy that cost us virtually nothing?

The best part—this kind of approach has long-lasting results. Once they came to the Well-Bred Cafe, they've kept on coming. Why? We did more than grab the attention of our target market. We tapped into the community, built community rapport, and delivered a memorable experience—one which extended to include quality food and a congenial atmosphere. Our perfect ending—bonds of loyalty that translate into continuing sales. Not just feted, but treated well, the new constituents of the Well-Bred Café want more of the same, and know where they can find it.

Whether you plan an occasional event, or make events the centerpiece of your marketing strategy, entertaining your target market gives you the opportunity to make connections, to increase your visibility, and to create goodwill. Make your event a memorable experience. Then make the most of it in your follow-through: networking and The Encore.

7. Tap Into Web Communities

Web communities generally represent an audience without metropolitan borders. But they are still a great way to tap into specific local communities who are following a specific cause. Howard Dean made United States presidential campaign history in his use of the internet to build a grassroots campaign against George Bush in 2003. His savvy tie-in with Meet Up (www.meetup.com) allowed individuals from all over the nation to hold monthly campaign support meetings and to promote awareness. In doing so, he minimized his expenditures on posters and direct mail, while maximizing his exposure to a target audience. Meet Up even allows members to post photographs and website links at no extra cost. Smart business owners, whose target market could be found in the local community of Dean Campaign supporters, signed up online and in so doing, also gained prime exposure within their individual city's entire Dean web community.

One of my earliest internet companies used to make a fortune selling products on eBay.com. eBay is an online auction site wherein anyone with something to sell can create an account and list their product. It seems that just about everything is listed on eBay. Homes, cars, electronics, antiques, books and even services are sold by the thousands each day. Because I found that over 50% of all New Human, Inc. web design customers had already attempted the "do it yourself" route, we started selling "do it yourself" web design books on eBay, coupled with an offer for web design services. Every 3 months, we would check in with the buyer and remind them of the design opportunity. This generated, over a 2-year period, over $26,000 worth of web design profits.

Most ideas, however, about using online communities to build networking contacts or to advertise to users are inadequately based on the commonly known tools: bulletin boards, chat rooms which are never used, email lists, etc. While it is true that these tools are effective, your best bet is to research web communities and find ones that are really active with minglers. Your goal is to find those which immediately establish an opportunity for live conversation and interaction. In other words, find online communities that will bring you to the attention of potential contacts/customers in your target market. These web communities offer an interface between the cyber world of the internet and the real world of your marketplace.

8. Create A Web Community Of Your Own

Websites. They are everywhere. I personally have designed hundreds of them. Websites are brilliant tools by which we can educate, sell, motivate, meet, distribute, buy, bargain, bid, barter, inspire, analyze, report and befriend. In community-oriented marketing, an effective website is a "must-have." But, as with any aspect of community-oriented marketing, you must first do your homework.

So, before you hire that so-called "web design company" to build a "website," make sure that you first set forth a clear vision of what you want to accomplish and how you intend your website to accomplish it. If you place this task in the hands of a web designer, you are almost certainly going to be headed for disaster. Map out your vision first! Then, and only then, find a web designer equipped to carry out that vision. This means an involved, finger-on-the-pulse professional who conceives of websites as specialized marketing tools. I encourage anyone interested in having a website to speak first with a marketing-savvy web company. This holds true whether you are building a more conventional business site or creating a community portal.

Now, having completed the initial process, you've developed a blueprint for a website that fulfills your commitment to community-oriented marketing. In the course of this process, you've decided that your ideal website is one that acts as a community portal and that creates your own web community. What steps do you now need to take to ensure that your site thrives and produces results?

Start by making a decision: Is your web community going to be local, regional or national? For the majority of all persons reading this book, the answer is local or regional.

Next, brainstorm ways to make your business website into a community-building tool. For that, your best resource is the internet itself. Research other sites. There are a lot of web communities out there to model. To get you started, here is a list of some of the most popular ones in my circles:

a.   www.ecademy.com—The United Kingdom's most comprehensive business community portal.

b.   www.linkedin.com—A United States business community portal.

c.   www.teachmeteamwork.com—A resource-rich community for educators, speakers and coaches.

d.   www.coachville.com—Another resource pool for professional coaches.

e.   www.craigslist.org—An enormous San Francisco based "home grown community site" for just about everything. (tip—don't model the design/layout, but use the content for ideas)

f.   www.anthonyrobbins.com/community—A community portal that is attached to the much larger website for Robbins Research, Inc.

As you explore these sites, take notes. Don't trust your memory—write the good ideas down, including why they stand out and why they work.

Now, take an incisive look at who makes up the community you wish to build on and invite through the doors of your internet portal. What needs can you fulfill? How can your web "ville" be a strong resource for them? If you are interested in attracting entrepreneurs, for example, what other organizations (which also cater to entrepreneurs) can you tie into your site?

Commit to spending a lot of time on your community web portal. Learn about e-books, forums, chat rooms, shopping carts, auto-responders, mailing lists and membership programs. Track down conferences or classes which address the subject from A to Z. You can even hire a web community coach who will guide you through the process (find this resource in Tom Heck's www. teachmeteamwork.com).

9. Create A Website That Acts As A Community Resource

Many marketers will agree that web communities are not for everyone. However, there are still ways to make the most of your website as a business building tool by leveraging community focus. For instance, the majority of businesses that do not need to create a web community can benefit by instead creating a website that is a *community resource.*

A community resource website should be one that is rich with usable, quotable information that is always changing in order to keep up with returning visitors. Do you remember earlier, when we talked about finding ways to separate yourself from the competition? A great way to accomplish this is to assert your organization as an authority on your industry or business focus. Here are some outstanding examples of community resource websites that support and empower a business or special interest group, even as they also achieve influential visibility for their respective originators.

- www.greenlife.com—A great example of how a business selling a product can combine a community portal with an e-commerce engine.

- www.developer.com—An information and support portal for technically oriented individuals.

- www.americancity.org—An excellent magazine which hosts information and articles on smart growth, urban planning and the future of American cities.

- www.ceosforcities.org—A nonprofit site with information which focuses on fostering positive competition amongst cities.

When planning out your own business website as a community resource, there are some important guidelines that you absolutely *must* keep in mind. For one, it's vital that people searching the web for industry-related information and articles are able to use your site as a research and development resource. For another, the media should also be able to quickly and easily obtain information from your website for reporting purposes. The bottom line: with this kind of site, having a navigable, user-friendly design is as critical as including great information and resources.

And what is the benefit of creating an accessible, easily navigated community resource website? What reward might you reap from all this planning? The answer: Sales. Potential customers will be more likely to sign up with a company that offers a wealth of fresh ideas and insight into their projects. In giving away relevant and current information, you have built confidence with your target market. You have also made an indelible impression of good will and helpfulness—you have earned gratitude. And, you are offering a resource that gives potential clients a reason to return to you on a regular basis—and *that* translates into marketable visibility. You are the one they will think of when they need your service or product.

More inspiration needed? In 2000, OnShore, Inc., a Chicago-based IT consulting firm, redeveloped www.onshore.com to better serve them as a business-building tech-community resource. When you visit their well-designed website, you get a lot more than the usual dull links for services and products. This site offers industry-related news, case studies, project summaries and technical briefs. When compared to the average technology consulting website, the outcome is clear: a resource site is more profitable than a brochure site.

Do you remember what I said earlier about emulating the star nonprofits as you design your business model? More than offering a stimulus for your focus on community, the most successful nonprofits also give a lesson in marketing dynamics that you can't ignore. The star nonprofits really shine when it comes to making connections and capitalizing on those connections. They know how to locate resources and how to use those resources to an optimal advantage. Take a look at one of the best examples of community resourcing you can find on the internet—and it comes from a nonprofit: Compass Point Nonprofit Services, www.compasspoint.org, America's leading nonprofit consulting, training and research organization, has a website that blows all competitors out of the water. There are so many tools and articles on every aspect of nonprofit development that it would take days to navigate the scope of the resources they offer online.

They also link to subsidiary web community portals for nonprofit officers, like trainingpoint.org and boardcafe.org.

Where do they go? What do they want? Why do they click? Whether you build a community portal, a community resource site or just a business brochure online, take your web presence seriously and track your results. A great way to track your results as a web marketer is to sign up with www.webstat.com. This service allows you to track when visitors enter your website, what they do once they get there, and which portions of your site are the most effective. For example, if someone enters my web page at www.sensiblecity.com and clicks on an article that I wrote, I know the article is ineffective if they spend less than one minute on the page that displays it. If a visitor spends 12 minutes reading an article and then clicks through to the "services" link (see example figure 2.1), I know that the article has sufficiently interested them in my business. I also know what linked websites and search engines are delivering users to my website and by what keywords. So before you hire a web design company, look for a marketing agency that knows how to leverage the internet for business growth or, alternatively, work with a professional who understands the importance of measuring progress for optimal results.

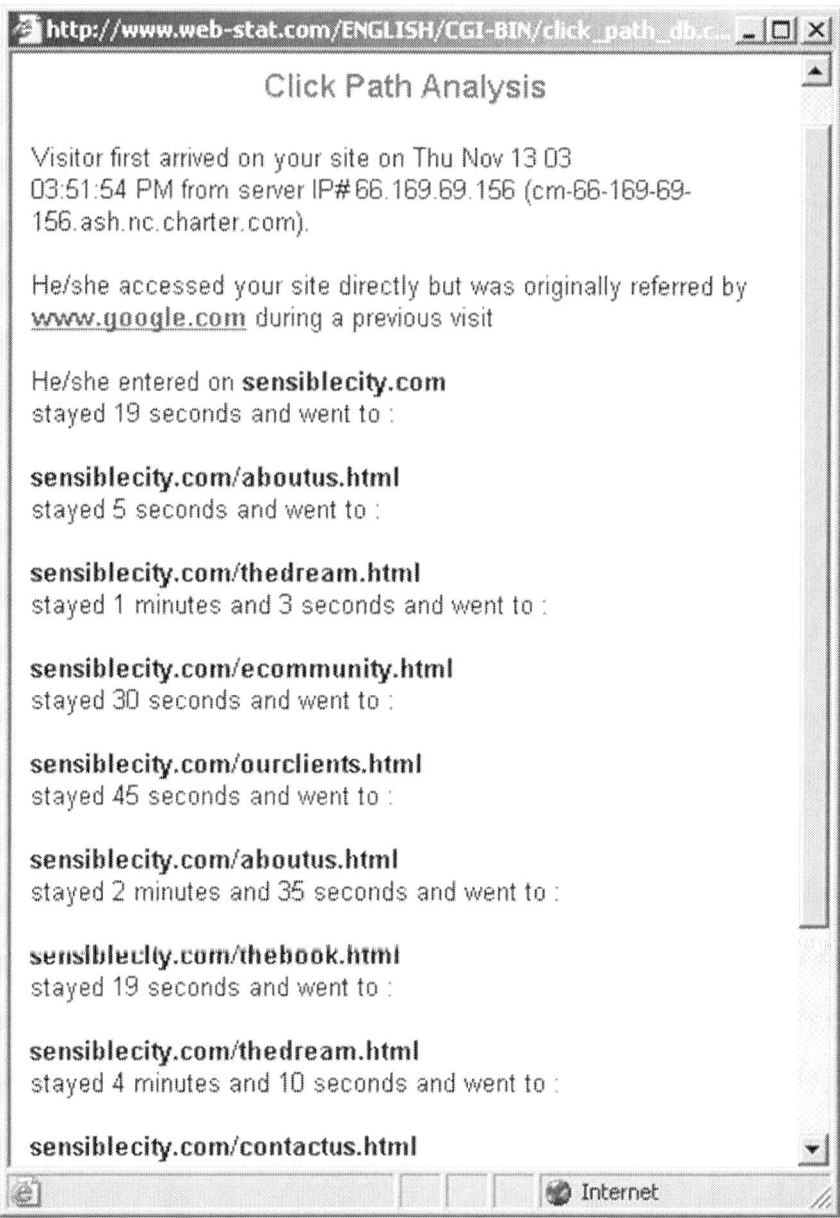

Figure 2.1: Web Tracking Example

Finally, notice that earlier I said an *effective* website. When I am considering working with any business, I check out their web page. It gives me the chance to see potential business relationships "with their pants down." If a website is cheaply built, I assume that the business is cheaply run. If a website is boring and un-resourceful, I expect the same of its proprietors. It doesn't matter whether your website is a traditional online store, or if it acts as a community portal. Whatever its purpose, it must be well-designed, content-relevant, up-to-date, inviting, and, in some way, notable. It should reflect you as a viable and productive business, and it should set you apart from the crowd in a positive, attractive way.

10. Network!

In most cases, rapid business growth by word of mouth begins with referrals. It is absolutely essential that you generate a cheerleading community who will inundate you with referrals. Networking is not something you do for a few hours each day when you go out to lunch. Networking is a way of life, centered on compassionate community consciousness. Do you remember Jeremiah Desmarais of Extremely Graphic Marketing? Several years ago, Jeremiah and I partnered on a project wherein my company provided web development for Kirk Tyson of Kirk Tyson International. Mr. Tyson is the unchallenged global authority on Competitive Intelligence in business. His business novel, *Competing In The 21st Century*, looks closely at the beneficial impacts of competition on our national and global marketplace. It teaches ethical ways of staying at the head of your field by monitoring industry practices and by keeping a constant focus on being one step ahead.

The first project Kirk invited us in on, was to design an intranet for a major insurance company. At the time, we had only represented smaller companies with less than 1,000 employees. I was thrilled by the magnitude of the project. The first question I asked myself after we left the meeting was, "What was the catalyst of that referral?"

It was all thanks to Jeremiah Desmarais, who was walking down Wells Street in Old Town one day when he passed a woman struggling with heavy boxes. Always ready to assist and empower, Jeremiah set down his briefcase and offered the woman a hand. As it turned out, she was the manager of an up-and-coming retail store called "Wholistic Living" that was just a few weeks away from a grand opening. Serendipitously, they were in need of a web designer for their store and Jeremiah quickly offered the name of my company, New Human. Kirk Tyson happened to be the owner of that store and thus the referral to a project with one of the largest insurance companies in the world. What is important to note here is that a cold-call selling web design services to Wholistic Living would never have resulted in that referral. Neither would a direct mail piece or an advertisement in The Chicago Tribune have generated the original web design job in the first place. New Human won that referral because Jeremiah Desmarais holds himself to the highest standards of community service from the time he leaves his apartment until the evening hour when he arrives back home.

I used to do a great deal of work in Chicago's City Hall. Again, a prestigious opportunity came through a simple referral. In 1998, I did some work for The Real Estate Education Company in downtown Chicago. While working with them, I made it a point to get to know everyone in their offices, even the people whose positions had no relevance to the job I was doing. I would invite them out to lunch and learn as much about them as I could. Years later, Sylvia Barrera, one of the employees of The Real Estate Education Company, called me out of the blue to offer me a referral. Her sister-in-law was an administrative assistant in the office of Alderman Ray Suarez. They needed someone to come in and build a custom software application. Again, that one referral meant a load of business projects at City Hall and a strong brand which I could brag about in my client list. But I didn't get into the epicenter of one of the largest cities on earth by marketing myself to them. I didn't get in by a cold call, direct mail, magazine advertisements or a press article. I got in because I had lunch with Sylvia Barrera.

Networking has different success rates for each type of business. Many networkers do 60-100% of all new business through networking referrals. Others network for years just to gain a few random referrals. And, there are those who give up after a while because they feel it is a waste of time. So, what will determine your success in networking?

When networking fails, it is usually because most networking organizations are dominated by people who join because they want to grow their business. Nothing is wrong with that. That's why we all join networking groups. But when it comes down to it, GETTING business is on the receiving end of someone else's action of GIVING you their resources. The failing component often arises when too many people are on the taking end. The solution? Select the right group and become a lovecat.

STEP ONE: SELECT THE RIGHT GROUP(S)

Watch out! Business networking is not about tapping into the biggest groups or the organizations with the most influence. The local chamber of commerce might not be right for your business. You are also likely to be faced with a slew of local competitors at many networking events. To sort it out ahead of time, first ask yourself what kind of people you want to get to know. Then, choose your group by following this model:

- Select a group that focuses on building strong personal relationships.
- Select a group with at least 60% business owners & entrepreneurs.
- Select a group that is small, but growing because of committed members.
- Select a group whose members are active in the community *outside* of their business activities.
- Most importantly, select a group of folks with big hearts so that Step Two can fall smoothly into place.

STEP TWO: BECOME A LOVECAT

Those of us who read voraciously about successful human relations know that GIVERS GAIN and TAKERS TAKE.

Hi, my name is Bob and I provide Such And Such service. I am looking for Such And Such business. Can you make me contacts? Make me rich? Can you give me your rolodex for the afternoon? Are you USEFUL to me?

There it is, in a nutshell. Takers take. In fact, when networking fails, it is usually because of two viruses:

1. **The Good Old Boy Flu**
   often brought on by: *bacteria passed through secret handshake*
   active viral strand: *Igiveyoubiz-Ifyougivemebiz*
   symptoms: *itching back, nausea from spastic smiling, emotional lethargy*

2. **The Sales-Minded Cold**
   often brought on by: *cash for brains condition*
   active viral strand: *gimme-gimme allyagot*
   symptoms: *overactive handshake, leading-questionitis, insinceritosis*

Do you remember Tim Sanders, whom I talked about earlier in this book? In his excellent book on personal business communication, *Love Is The Killer App*, Sanders offers that success in business is contingent upon your compassionate ability to share your knowledge and to project honest human warmth as you make your circles. This is what Sanders terms being a *lovecat*. For myself, in networking, to become a lovecat means getting out of the ME Frame and into the WE Frame. In the WE Frame, you focus 80% of your energy into empowering the others in your networking group. Forget about what they can do for you. Forget about who they know or where they go. Ask only of yourself, "What can I do to make this person more fulfilled?"

Underlying this message is—once again—*attraction*, the driving dynamic of community-oriented marketing in *all* its aspects. The principle behind this kind of networking is the same one we've discussed before—what you give out comes back to you, full circle. This is, of course, why sales-minded, money-hungry business owners and executives who attempt to exploit networking environments purely for personal gain are in danger of failure.

To successfully play this model out, you must recognize two separate, yet connected things—that you are growing your business by empowering others, and that inherent in the act of giving is the humbling of the self. Take a moment, and contemplate what this means. To make this approach work, you must believe, and practice this belief. This comes from the inside out—from the heart. Remember—your intention is held within your action. *Your intention* is the seed you are planting. Whatever harvest you reap grows out of it.

And how do you put the model to work? A good place to start is by asking yourself, "What do I have to offer?" Then, whatever your answer is, give it away. Do you provide a service for a fee? Give it away for one hour to anyone in your group who wants to listen and is serious about doing business.

There's one other essential to networking success—if you wish to succeed at it, you must always be doing it. There's more to networking, by the way, than shaking hands and striking up conversations over mutual interests. Be savvy—focus on people who know other people. Who are the real connectors in the community? Create an organizational system and schedule a time each week for following up with telephone calls and cards. Make an effort to spend a little bit of time with every person you meet and, if possible, send them some business. When developing your 12-month community-oriented marketing plan, establish a once-per-month focus on finding new groups and outlets for expanding your network base. Here are some organizations you may want to check out as you're generating ideas:

- Your Area Chamber of Commerce

- Rotary International (www.rotary.org)

- Business Network International (www.bni.com)

- Fast Company's "Company Of Friends" (www.fastcompany.com/cof)
- Networlding (www.networlding.com)
- Itsnotwhatyouknow, LLC (www.itsnotwhatyouknow.com)

11. Start Your Own Group

No networking groups in your area? Can you assume a leadership role? If so, then think about starting your own networking group. You'll need to contact at least ten business owners you know and ask them if they would be interested in meeting regularly to pass on qualified referrals (most will express interest immediately). Meet weekly or monthly for at least 1 hour (usually around a meal) and plan your meeting as follows:

1. Open the meeting formally and follow an agenda. Establish roles and elect a president or chairman to moderate the meeting.

2. Have each member stand up and introduce themselves and their business. Each member should be specific ("A good referral for me is…") about what they want.

3. After the members speak, give visitors and potential new members the opportunity to do the same.

4. For each meeting, have one member of the group perform a 10-15 minute presentation to introduce their business and invite questions.

5. Towards the end, pass referrals. Create a paper system for tracking who is passing referrals and follow up to make sure that the referrals being passed are genuine.

6. To make sure that your group is successful:

    - Pass a card filing system around the room so that each member can insert, remove and share business cards.

    - Focus on giving referrals rather than hunting for leads.

    - Be selective and only vote new members in whose values and businesses resonate with the whole of your group.

    - According to research conducted by Business Networking International, the most successful referral groups are those with more than 25 members. Hold regular social events to attract visitors and potential members. Make a goal of increasing membership by at least 4 persons per month.

- Establish individual and group goals to keep everyone motivated.

- Have fun! Make sure that your networking group is an energetic and productive one that each member looks forward to attending.

Networking is not just about attending focused groups, either. In your local newspaper or independent weekly, you can find networking opportunities all over town. Nonprofit fundraisers, art openings, classes and lectures, merchant associations and even neighborhood associations are great places to start. Pay close attention to every detail of your outside world.

If you don't know how to talk to people, hire a professional coach or join a group like Toastmasters™. If you don't know how to meet people, get creative. I know a network administrator who built his business by riding an elevator. Jacob Orloff of Atlanta's Lanscorp Technologies would go to high rise office buildings in the affluent district of Buckhead and simply ride the elevator, creating conversation with anyone who would listen. He would dress like an executive in order to gain respect from the executives on the elevator. Jacob drummed up a few clients a week this way, riding the elevators in different buildings, sometimes for as long as 4 hours. Nowadays, he probably would be arrested for suspicion, but in 1996, the elevator was his open road to opportunity.

All around you, day and night, you are surrounded by individuals who can, by leveraging their own contact base, make you very successful. What creative route will you take to meet them?

12. Let Others Market Through You

I know coffee shop owners who send out coupons in the CPA's invoice envelopes. I know grocery stores that allow massage therapists to setup a massage chair for customers during rush hour. How can you be an advertisement for a colleague whose business targets your customer market? This is one of the easiest ways to be a hero in your business community.

I am sure you have noticed that I am a believer in professional coaching. As a marketer, I find that many professionals are in need of a supportive partner who can help them define their goals and identify opportunities that will make those goals happen. Establishing this kind of relationship with another businessperson is one of the ways I give of myself in the networking process. When my company sends out its monthly billing, we include promotions from a few local coaches whom I believe in. It works wonders for these coaches and in turn, they often refer business to my company.

I also work with many clients who are building out new offices, purchasing technological equipment, setting up computer networks and buying furniture. As a good neighbor in the local business community, I am a walking advertisement for the community-oriented businesses that provide these services. Acting as a primary connection between businesses increases my own network visibility and results in hefty referrals from grateful service providers.

Making referrals as a part of your networking strategy is an easy way of marketing yourself, and it doesn't cost a cent. Simply make a list of 10 businesses who would love to market themselves to your clientele. Then contact them and ask for a flyer, brochure or stack of business cards. Whenever possible (remember The Encore?), identify needs in your own client base which match the offerings of your colleagues. When you find a match, make the referral. Congratulations! You just empowered an established or potential client with an important resource and made a sales professional's day. Warning: only enact this strategy with colleagues whose integrity and community values match yours. A referral to poor businesses is a reflection upon yourself!

13. Conduct Wise Trades, Geared Towards Generating Referrals

How can you turn a no-cash trade into a profitable referral? In small business circles and even amongst monstrous corporations, bartering offers are to be expected. There are many different opinions on this matter. Some marketing advisors will tell you to never, under any circumstances, "devalue" your product or service by bartering or trading it away. And yet I'll bet that there is not a radio station in the civilized world that doesn't put the barter process into action. I suggest that you carefully analyze each offer and utilize only one system:

1. Identify your possible trade relationship for its potential to generate additional business. How? By determining the target market and contact sphere of your colleague that is interested in the trade.

2. If the trade relationship shows strong potential for future referrals, clearly communicate that your trade is contingent upon a referrals-based business relationship.

3. If the trade relationship does not show strong potential for future referrals, offer a partial trade that will insure your costs are met.

4. On occasion, listen to your gut and conduct compassionate, irrational trades.

When I met with Melissa Gobbi, a yoga instructor in Asheville, I knew The Sensible City's web design fees would be unrealistic for her business. But my instincts told me that offering her a trade would be mutually beneficial. The Sensible City's client base is dominated by socially responsible professionals, and many of them have a clear personal focus on having abundant health and vitality. Additionally, I have a great admiration for entrepreneurs who choose to make a living by empowering others. In Melissa's case, by teaching yoga, she is able to help individuals achieve high levels of personal health and add years to their lifespan. I accepted her offer to trade and asked, very specifically and directly, if she would focus on creating quality referrals in exchange. Within one year, The Sensible City had completed 3 client projects based on referrals generated from our trade with Melissa. The process was simple—she would encourage everyone in her classes to visit the site. Later she would ask people if they liked it and if so, offer information about her experience with my company.

Trading can also be a great way to generate advertising without the drain on your bank account. If you provide a service or product that is in demand by any kind of media outlet, contact someone in charge and offer a trade. In many situations, over 25% of all advertising you encounter in the media is based on trades. This is what I mean by conducting *wise trades, geared towards generating referrals.* What are some ways that you can use trades to increase referrals? Be sure to focus on contact spheres (we'll talk more about contact spheres in Section 3 of this book) and client markets. You will find that conducting trades can be very profitable.

14. Send Thank You Notes

A sincere and personalized thank-you note can do more for your business than the flashiest brochure in town. No advertisement or product placement can compare to the warm fuzzy you can generate by simply appreciating people. What is really amazing about this is that this simple little action is only practiced by a small minority of professionals. Think about it. How many people did you meet with last year who sent you a note of thanks? Of the professionals who did, how many sent you a dull, sales-minded thank-you note?

Set yourself apart. Buy thank-you notes from the store or have a stationary engraver create them for your business. Hand-write every single note you send out and be specific. If you had lunch with someone you met in your networking group, send them a note to let them know how much you appreciated the conversation. Point out their strengths, and if you learned something from them, thank them for the lesson. The key to success in note-writing is sincerity and punctuality. Send out thank-you notes each week on the same day. Keep a running list of "who and why" throughout the week and make sure you catalog mailing addresses from business cards.

Don't limit your thanks to prospective clients and customers, either. Thank colleagues, upstream providers, professionals whom you buy from, the mail carrier, etc. Look for ways to surprise people with gratitude. When you meet someone who makes a positive or inspiring impression, send them a book that made a strong impact on you. And here's a creative twist on this easy little marketing strategy—one that can do wonders for your web community. If you have an information-driven website, you should be able to find space on it for a public announcement about their business. Include a link for your visitors to check them out. After you've done this, send them a card, letting them know that, because you want them to succeed, you are taking this simple action as an act of gratitude.

Again, sincerity is everything. Come from the heart and use your own words. Don't send out a card that says, "Thank you for a stimulating conversation. I look forward to serving your business in the future." Instead, try something more like: "Wow, what a great lunch! I really enjoyed our conversation. I can't wait to see how this relationship develops."

15. Create A Volunteer Program Or Volunteer Yourself

Looking for an easy way to empower specific communities and gain media attention in the process? Create a volunteer program and develop a strategic action plan for implementing it in the community. Here's a model to follow:

1. Consult your research into nonprofit communities that are linked up with your target market and who are in need of volunteers. We'll talk about the research phase later in this book.

2. Assess your staff (or yourself if you are a lone entrepreneur) for strengths and weaknesses which would determine effectiveness in a volunteer environment.

3. Talk to your entire company or even your networking group about volunteering as a team effort, rather than individual volunteering.

4. Whatever you do, don't over-commit yourself. It is more damaging to volunteer and not show up than it is to not volunteer at all. Make a decision and keep your commitments. If your staff does not show interest in volunteering, don't try to force them.

5. Do your research. There are many groups out there in need of volunteers that you may not have considered. Here are a few ideas:

    - Urban beautification and community gardening projects
    - Public schools and universities
    - Homeless shelters and orphanages
    - Senior citizen retirement homes
    - Community theatres and performing arts companies
    - Prisons and rehabilitation centers
    - Galleries and museums
    - Community centers and organizations which support youth
    - Literacy projects and organizations
    - Many, many more.

Be passionate about volunteering! Make sure that anyone who volunteers under your business name shows up with a great attitude and a sense of humor. And commit to a timeline. It is best to encourage once-monthly volunteer activity. If you commit to weekly activity, make sure that you can make appointments.

Whether you do business alone or manage a staff of thousands, part of your job as a hero in the community is to create a volunteer program and spark some noticeable activity in your community. Do you remember The Starbuck's Foundation? What are some ways that your business can serve the community? What are some ways that you can reward your staff for getting out there and making a difference?

16. Festivals, Trade Shows And Fairs

Festivals, trade shows and fairs funnel large groups of people into a staged area, most of them looking for entertainment or a particular product/service. I recently signed up 6 Sensible City clients in the same street festival. It was called "Organicfest" and the cost of a booth at the event was a staggeringly low $56.

The producers of the festival wanted to get as many sponsors as possible, so they allowed non-food businesses to get involved, as long as they did not sell any products that were conventionally made. For my clients whose target market was health-conscious individuals, this was a great opportunity. Here I reference one of the most difficult professions to market—chiropractors. While it seems that 9 in 10 marketing efforts for my chiropractor tendered poor results, setting him up at a street festival achieved a 1,000 % plus return on investment. And while my chiropractor was signing up potential practice members as fast as his little tent could process them, 2 out of 6 of my other clients enjoyed little more than a good case of sunburn.

What makes the difference? I could write an entire book on public display appearances alone. But here are some tips for participating in public events for optimum results. They apply to festivals, tradeshows and fairs.

- Play full out—don't just set up a table, then sit back in your chair. Stand up! Engage the community. Have the best-looking setup you can possibly put together. Print a large, full color banner or sign and make sure that it is visible.

- When deciding what events to get involved in, get creative in your research. I know an architect who sets up a booth at her local Renaissance Faire.

- If you are outdoors, fill a cooler with bottled water and offer it to anyone who approaches your booth.

- Always have at least one contest for an item of universal value. Buy a cruise package, computer, gift certificate or, if on a budget, a gift basket, and hold a drawing at the end of the day (this generates a mailing list as well as a reason to have participants return to your booth later on).

- Get help. Never, ever set up a booth by yourself. Get 2, if not 3 individuals involved. If you are introverted, make sure you have an extrovert with you who will engage passers-by and draw them in.

- Network with other booth-holders. More often than not, you can find clients lurking behind their tables. Scan the event and look for opportunities to cross-promote and cross-market.

- Smile. Dress comfortably, but well. Put on your best attitude and project it forward. Buy flowers and put them on your table or come up with an attractive gimmick. In other words, attract!

17. Nonprofit Empowerment Activities

Growing your business through the active empowerment of nonprofit organizations whose member base consists largely of your target audience is a core "must-do" if you wish to attract values partners in the community. There is, though, a lot of argument in the marketing community about this highly misunderstood topic. The argument comes from the misconception that nonprofit sponsorship is about creative check writing, which results in a wide array of static logo placements.

Sponsorship has come a long way in recent years. To see how far, let's first take a look to the past. Overall, the concept of sponsorship as a business development model has been an active idea in marketing for about 40 years. In its infancy, sponsorship produced only slight results because:

- Sponsoring businesses would assume profile relationships with nonprofits that did not accurately represent their target market.

- Sponsorships would focus on establishing a bond with the event, the organization or activity without building and nurturing a relationship with their target market.

- Businesses would place sponsorship as a tail-end marketing activity, focusing less management and smart planning on their sponsorships than they focused on their mainstream marketing projects.

- Businesses would coordinate all sponsorship through a mid-level marketing executive, rather than a top-level creative professional.

In more recent years we have watched as sponsorship evolved into an overwhelming series of random logo placement campaigns. The chances are, you have been to special events that had a dozen logos listed as active sponsors. Yet it is unlikely you can easily recall more than 4 of them. And of the ones you can recall, what usually comes to mind is a brand with which you have no emotional connection. Businesses serious about sponsorship might want to check out *The Sponsor's Toolkit,* by Anne-Marie Grey and Kim Skildum-Reid. Although geared towards big business spenders, this book provides exciting insight into the multidimensional potential of a well thought-out sponsorship campaign. It also offers a road map for avoiding and out-maneuvering common sponsorship pitfalls that could cost you money.

Forget about what you've seen and heard. Nonprofit empowerment is tangible, quantifiable and dramatic in potential. It is the most emotional and values-inspired of all marketing media. For all these reasons, your uplifting support of the right nonprofit should be handled like it is a marketing campaign all to its own. So let's look at ideas and ways to make sponsorship one of the shining focal points of your marketing plan.

The first major step in nonprofit empowerment is to choose and choose wisely. Be careful about working with national nonprofit organizations that are over organized. One of my clients who owns a restaurant in Memphis, Tennessee asked me to advise her on how to set up a fundraiser for her favorite nonprofit. When I telephoned the organization and spoke with their public relations director about hosting a fundraiser at a high profile restaurant, the response I received was: "I am sorry, but we don't do fundraisers with just anyone. I'll have to raise this with the board next month." Beware of these over managed organizations. Don't chase after them! Instead find one that will bend over backwards to court you as a sponsor.

Here are my criteria for selecting the ideal nonprofit:

- Make sure that the organization *really needs* help. All nonprofits say that they really need help. But find one which needs it enough to court *your* interests as well as their own.

- Look for the local organizations that are strong in the community and are eager to work creatively with a business in order to create maximum benefits for mutual gain.

- Make darned sure that the organization you are sponsoring possesses your target market as its primary member support base.

- Look at their activities in the community. Make sure that they have a highly social calendar.

- Analyze their communication practices and social approach. Are they delivering a memorable, emotional experience to their member base/audience? (If everything else falls into place but this item, and you feel committed to the organization's goals and ideals, volunteer to teach them this as a part of your sponsorship.)

- Offer to buy the company director lunch or a cup of coffee and compare notes. Consider their personality and ask yourself whether or not you want to create a long-term partnership with this person.

- Make sure that the organization has a marketing strategy for growth and a geographic focus which matches your own.

Once you have selected your nonprofit organization(s) to work with, here are some ideas to get your imagination going.

- Sponsorship is the most holistic of all marketing approaches. Make sure that you integrate your values-based message to the community across as many media as possible.

- Find ways to use your business name and, if you have one, location, to create dramatic community recognition and financial growth for the organization over a period of time.

- Rather than make an enormous annual donation, choose instead to host fundraisers, themed events and business networking socials that will benefit your nonprofit partner. In other words, become a primary figure in your nonprofit partner organization's growth by way of your active and attentive presence throughout the year.

- Leverage your relationships with other community-minded businesses and invite them to join you for sponsorship projects and events. If you attend a business networking event, invite the head of your nonprofit partner with you as a guest. Introduce him or her to the members of your group as a great marketing opportunity, and invite them to join you in sponsorship.

- Use the media to your full advantage. Always be on the lookout for ways to create an original story with an unusual or intriguing angle. Use the media to involve and inform the community in every aspect of your nonprofit sponsorships.

- Keep in mind that you are, in fact, marketing your nonprofit, using the same techniques and concepts with which you market yourself. This is what, in the community-marketing pantheon, re-invents sponsorship and takes it to a new level.

Focus on events that deliver an emotionally memorable experience and become a synergistic part of that energy. One of the biggest mistakes I have too often seen sponsors make in the past has been their attempts to actually divert the audience's attention from the experience they are having. This is a terribly harmful approach that can backfire on the sponsor. It can even build brand resentment. Remember that you want your business to be welcome into the personal lives of every person involved. Your attitude and your presentation reflect on your own business, as well as affect your nonprofit's success. So, whether you step up to the mike, are sharing a table, or are working your way through the crowd, keep in mind that you are usually communicating to people who are "off the clock." Make them smile, laugh, sing a song. Make them a part of the event. Just make sure, on the other hand, that you don't bombard them with a commercial when they are trying to relax and have fun.

The Sensible City, from time to time, produces major social events and musical concerts. It's a great way to both give back to the community and simultaneously market ourselves. It's also an opportunity to create my favorite type of event—community-oriented catalyst events. When planning these events, I line up a wide array of our own clients and a select group of community-minded business owners to create an overwhelming, electrifying and emotional experience. For Joshua Singing Tree's 2003 concert, "Adawehi", I was thrilled to actually MC the show. Joshua, a brilliant musician and raving fan of community consciousness, allowed me to say whatever I wanted in the opening. So I stepped up to the microphone and let the audience know that the only reason why the evening they were about to experience was possible was because of the generous support of businesses who were committed to making the arts possible and profitable in their city. Before I could finish speaking, the audience burst into a round of applause. I then directed them to please read the programs from cover to cover and make note of those kind businesses who had offered their support.

But that's not all. The event, which was carefully promoted through consistent media releases and a citywide grassroots poster campaign, had been eagerly anticipated throughout town, and had even become a buzzword in some communities. At the concert, premier sponsors were allowed to set up tables and distribute information in the lobby. Sponsors were again recognized on the website and in the press. Fortunately, Joshua and his fellow performers on stage put on a production that spawned only positive acclaim. 6 months after the event I was still running into people who had been inspired by it and who were, as a result, doing business with one or more of the sponsors.

The moral of the story is that when managing a sponsorship campaign you need to step out of the box and send it off to the recycling bin. However, not every nonprofit director will be receptive to your progressive suggestions. So look for a development director with an imagination. Then, be as creative and original as your own imagination will allow. Better yet, stretch your imagination. For instance, tie together unlikely nonprofits and businesses. I know of a theatre company who joined forces with Life Blood for the opening night of their "Dracula" premier. In one night, that teaming up and the press they received because of it more than tripled the exposure of the theatre company's sponsorship community!

To be really effective, your sponsorship should be a part of your 12-month marketing plan. Your plan should also include a monthly focus on a less prominent nonprofit sponsorship. For example, I know of an office supply store that gives away a $100 gift certificate to the winners of 6 golf tournaments per year, each tournament benefiting a different nonprofit. Because the golf community in his city is dominated by businesspeople, he is roping in his target market with little difficulty and little cost. Yet, for these efforts, the corresponding exposure he receives is broad in its potential.

There can, by the way, be much more to nonprofit empowerment than the comprehensive business sponsorship model. If you have a retail business, you are likely to be regularly bombarded with various requests for donations. I encourage my retail clients to make a counter offer. Instead of writing a check for their minimum amount, offer to host a single fundraiser or community awareness event. If well planned and promoted, the event would tender much more than your simple check and it would be a win-win situation for all parties involved. This, obviously, is an ideal way to get involved if you're not yet up to taking on a more elaborate commitment. Just remember to use the same criteria listed earlier for selecting your nonprofit. The concerns are the same, as is the goal—a mutually beneficial, empowering relationship.

18. Get Published

This is primarily thought of as an option for consultants, educators, speakers and industry gurus. But it can work for many, many other kinds of businesses. For example, a restaurant, once it has established its clientele, can sell cookbooks. Whatever your industry focus, publishing a book or even a column in the local paper can mean landslide results if done right. Many books have been written on this subject and there is a wealth of information to be found online. You'll need to consider the pros and cons of large publishers, small presses and self-publishing. You will also need to learn about when and if an agent is optional and, if you need an agent, how to find one. My only suggestion is to start small. Talk with community newspapers and work your way up to mainstream publications. If your focus is on creating a book, read similar books on the market until you have a clear vision of what you can write about that is better and different from anything else out there.

There are many ways to increase the odds of successful publication, so do your homework and have fun. Writing can be a very rewarding process. However, just as I mentioned earlier when discussing radio, I encourage you to make sure that you are delivering a needed resource to the community. For your writing to have impact, it mustn't be an ego-log. Ask yourself: "What do I have to give and how can I deliver it as a community resource?"

19. Empower Others As A Daily Practice

It is so easy to make somebody's day. No matter where you go, you are always meeting and interacting with people who could benefit from a positive boost in their lives. Do you remember what I said earlier about thank-you notes? That is just the tip of the iceberg when building a plan for people-empowerment. If you make a habit of connecting with at least one other person each day and improving upon their mental health, you will propel yourself forward as a professional faster than by all of the other tactics listed in this section. So keep track of birthdays and anniversaries. Send a grieving colleague a bouquet of flowers. Buy books that will empower your fellow professionals and mail them out as gifts. Apply this to your networking plan and create mind maps for generating business for your friends, colleagues and clients. Make it a part of your morning preparation when you are laying out your to-do lists. Who can I reach out to and empower today?

"We have a choice to use the gift of our lives to make the world a better place."

—Dr. Jane Goodall

PART IV

Create a 12-Month Action Plan for Growth

Your First Steps

Josie Williams of Fastball Liquidation Services looked exasperated. Her marketing director wanted my company to represent them on a consulting level. Josie's hesitation was that she just couldn't justify the expense, based on her notions of what marketing is all about. We had been through the loops of proposals and follow-ups and now it was time for her to make a decision. She took off her glasses, leaned over her desk with an expression of total confidence and stated, "I'm an entrepreneur. I built my business from the ground up and even now, after seven years, I am *always* marketing. What do *I* need a long-range marketing plan for? I have a marketing department. I have plenty of marketing books. Can't I just hire you to organize a few community-oriented marketing *projects* and achieve the same results?"

It may be that you, too, are on the verge of the same question. And if you are among those who feel they don't need a long-range plan, it's not surprising. Most businesses turn to marketing when they get uncomfortable. When Siteleader.com was processing hundreds of orders a day for web hosting back in 1999, they would have laughed had I suggested that they invest time and money into building a long-range plan for sustainable growth. But one year later, as their customers were taking business to the competition in hoards, Siteleader started talking about a long-range marketing plan. And guess what: the competitors that were winning over Siteleader's customers were acting out their own long-term aggressive marketing campaigns.

Anyone who has ever experienced the application process for an SBA loan knows that a business plan is required and that the most scrutinized section is your financial projections, followed by your action plan for sustainable growth. Believe it or not, the SBA isn't trying to give you a hard time. Committing funds to financial growth should be accompanied by the business-owner's demonstrable commitment to the same. Growing a business requires attention to the details and it requires planning. A good corollary to the importance of a long-range marketing plan can be found in higher education. Without the systematic process of classes, semesters and academic years, taking in all of the necessary information in order to achieve a degree would be overwhelming and chaotic. The achievement is entirely dependent upon an intentional structure for progressive growth.

If you, though, are ready to get started as a community-oriented business, then you're also ready to commit to the steps necessary to achieve definable success. And that most definitely means your developing a viable and organized plan of action, grounded in the principles we've been discussing throughout this book.

So, let's get down to business. The best way to put your own long-range plan together is to use the step-by-step model that follows. I suggest, as you follow this model, that you develop your identity pieces while simultaneously researching your communities and creating contacts. If you address these two projects at once, they can be planned to reach fruition and tie in together at the same time. The following page offers a diagram for you to follow along.

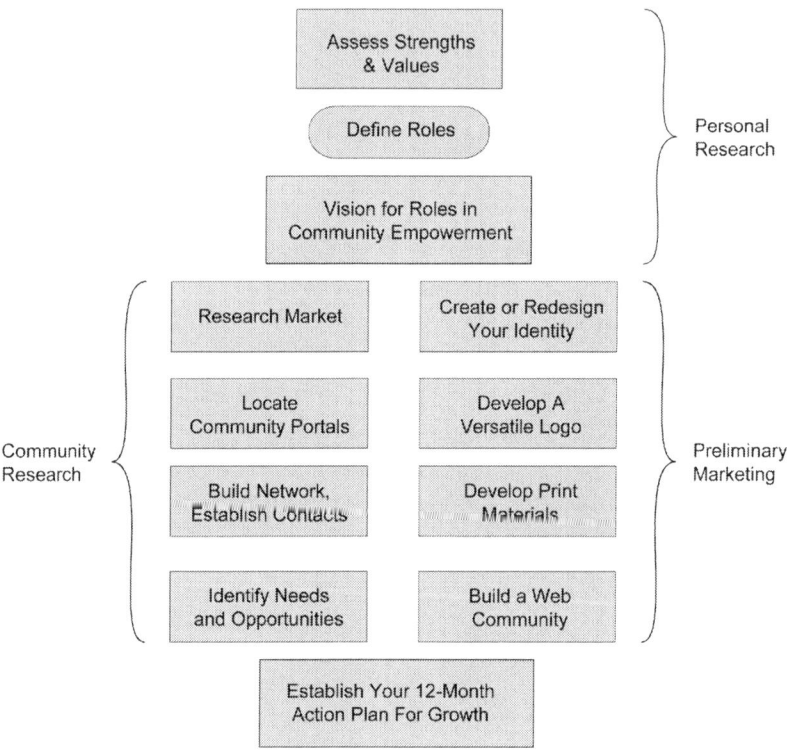

Figure 3.1—Creating Your Marketing Plan

Assess Your Strengths And Put Them To Work

As you can see in figure 3.1, the first task at hand when building your plan is a self-assessment of strengths. This can apply to an individual or a company of 1,000. Are you influential? Connected? Are you a great communicator or leader? Are you good at managing projects and getting things done? This list doesn't have to sensibly tie directly in with marketing. Just start listing as many resources and strengths—personal and/or business—as possible. Commit yourself to creating a list of 100 strengths that you can put into action in your marketing plan. If you are working with a team or a sales force, ask the same of each of them. The reason for doing this is so you don't create a plan that calls upon your weaknesses. If you don't work well in groups, you don't want to foist an identity of "teacher" upon yourself. If you prefer to manage a program rather than design it, then you won't want to step up to the plate as a "project planner."

Here are the first 15 of my 100 strengths I listed when brainstorming what strengths my business could put to work in my community-oriented marketing plan:

1. I personally love to educate.

2. Our office is easy to find downtown and can be used as an educational or otherwise gathering space.

3. I work well as a chairperson with boards of directors.

4. I am a decent writer and can influence others with words.

5. I understand how to integrate marketing and web design into one component.

6. I enjoy nature and outdoor activities.

7. My staff and I are all big fans of local performing arts.

8. I have a state of the art computer network with high-speed printing capabilities.

9. I know how to prepare sushi.

10. I carry the power to influence certain groups of people.

11. I am well-connected through many formal and informal networking channels.

12. I know decision-makers and politicians in city government.

13. My business partner used to do corporate training.

14. My executive assistant is a marathon runner.

15. I am an excellent organizer and planner.

Based on this list, I can clearly put a number of these strengths to work, both in the community and in the implementation & management of my own marketing plan. The key to narrowing down your strengths and identifying their use in the community is to establish roles. That becomes your next step in creating your long-range plan of action.

Establishing Your Roles In The Community

Instead of sorting through hundreds of techniques for community empowerment, focus in first on the best roles which suit your taste, and then decide what techniques match your roles. For example, if you have important information to share that makes a strong impact or provides an emotional experience, be an Educator in your community. If, however, you are stage-shy, perhaps it would be better to simply host other educators in your space and be a Host/Entertainer. To follow are the primary roles that you might assume in community-oriented marketing. The ideal approach is to pick two or three of these roles. If you have a small, clearly defined target market, two roles is plenty. If you have a department store, go with three.

Ideal Roles:

Educator—Empower your communities with important, in-demand information. This includes presenting, writing, coaching and more.

Caretaker—Empower your communities with volunteer efforts and urban renewal projects that improve your target market's lives. As well, a caretaker role can include involvement in substantive environmental programs, hospices and more.

Motivator/Catalyst—Get people together and start something big that will make your community a better place.

Leader/Pioneer—Assume and enact a leadership role with an organization which provides high visibility to your target market.

Host/Entertainer—Use your place of business or organize a space to host other educators, caretakers, motivators and leaders in their empowerment activities.

Connector—Become a referral & networking maven in your target market's communities.

The Sensible City's activities in the community are focused through the roles of Educator, Motivator/Catalyst and Connector. Some examples of strengths that tie in with these roles are listed as follows:

Educator	Motivator/Catalyst	Connector
I personally love to educate.	I work well as a chairperson with boards of directors.	I carry the power to influence certain groups of people.
I am a writer and can influence others with words.	I am an excellent organizer and planner.	I am well connected through many formal and informal networking channels.
My business partner used to do corporate training.		

While assessing your strengths, be sure to also take an honest inventory of your weaknesses. Here, too, you need to be systematic and disciplined. Make a list just as you did when identifying the strengths/resources of yourself and of your business. When assessing the items on this list, keep in mind that your weaknesses can potentially lead you into activities and roles that have a negative outcome. As a result, you may end up with a poor reputation within the community you have targeted. For example, if you have a hard time saying no, create a communications strategy that will protect you from assuming a Donor role. If, conversely, you don't assess this weakness and address it, you may end up overextending yourself with unrealistic commitments, and become known as an unreliable no-show.

Aside from your own weaknesses, then, there are also some weak roles. These are negative roles that can inflict major wounds in your marketing plan and in some cases, even generate bad press about your business.

Roles To Avoid: Martyr—"I work so hard to help people and nobody cares."

Donor—"I am an open door for donation requests."

Butterfly—"This didn't make me any money, so I am off to the next garden of flowers."

The Butterfly role is the most dangerous as well as the most common. If you are going to get involved in a community empowerment project, commit yourself fully and detach from the results. Backing out or reducing the stakes halfway into a project because you are not experiencing the financial gains you intended can build strong enemies in the community and in the end, cost you more. This is why laying the groundwork for any project should begin with knowing yourself and relating that knowledge to what it is you want to accomplish. Otherwise, you will sabotage your efforts, and will probably blame the other guy, to boot. What are your roles and how will your strengths support them?

Role # 1:	Role # 2:	Role # 3 (optional):
Strengths:	Strengths:	Strengths:

Create A Vision For Your Roles
In Community Empowerment

Most businesses are encouraged to create a mission statement that expresses their vision as part of their business plan. I personally detest reading most of these mission statements and visions, mainly because the majority of businesses don't stand by them. So when I suggest that you create a Vision for your roles in community empowerment, think of it as though you are creating a garment that you will wear out in public each day. Your vision is a clear projection of what you stand for and what you are going to create. Your mission statement puts your vision out front for everyone else to see. Is it a good fit?

Here is an excerpt of our Vision from The Sensible City's long-range marketing plan:

Vision:

> The Sensible City *educates, motivates* and *integrates* key players in urban society, enabling them to build a stronger community which benefits all.
> We educate and inspire professionals from all walks of life by leveraging our experience in corporate training and our passion for the distribution of empowering information.
> We inspire positive change and motivate leaders to raise the bar on their organizational growth. As key planning experts, we seek out creative opportunities to empower groups which are in need of our management support to foster needed growth.
> We are human and organizational resource brokers, facilitating strong connections amongst people, groups, businesses, nonprofits and government organizations. We do this by connecting people to people, one introduction at a time on a grassroots level.

Now it's time for you to jump in. What are your roles and how do you envision yourself delivering them? Are you a landscaping company that focuses on environmentally responsible projects (Caretaker)? Or maybe you are a coffeehouse owner who wants to host literacy projects and underground arts (Educa-tor—Host)? Whatever your profession, you should be able to create a vision for how you are going to apply your roles in the communities you focus on.

Create Or Redesign Your Identity As A Community-Oriented Business

Do you have one of those logos that just kind of makes a swirl around a word and that's it? Do you have a real estate company that shows nothing more than a house for a logo? Maybe you have a travel business and your logo is an image of a cruise ship. I am not going to advise you to spend more money than you need to. But if your logo stinks, you already know it. If that's the case, and you have been considering a redesign, make the moment work for you. Come up with a design that reflects your professional abilities and gives some indication of your community focus.

Design is important. How you look on paper and online really does affect your business. If you don't believe me, look around. The best-looking companies are more often than not the most successful. So, take advantage of this stage in your plan for long-range growth. Put some thought into your identity pieces. How can they best reflect what you are about? What effect will they have on your target market—the customers you want to draw to yourself? While you're at it, consider all the different possibilities. Do you have a generic invoice from an office supply store? If you're having business cards and stationery designed, how about creating an invoice that's yours alone, too. Finally, invest as much as you can. Your identity pieces are a reflection of you. A boring business card, or a flyer that looks like it was made by a grade-schooler, will send out a negative message, one that's bad for your business.

On the issue of investment, whether you need to redesign your image or you're starting out, it's a smart idea to spin off your identity design project to a professional. Don't, though, just randomly pick your designer out of the phone book. Network around town until you find another business that looks great. Ask them for a referral to their designer. Then research any and all referrals. Make sure, no matter where you find him/her, that the designer you work with understands marketing. Whenever possible, use a marketing agency that focuses on producing quality design as part and parcel of their marketing business. Avoid, as much as you can, having separate designers for separate pieces. When one design firm does it all, your final look will show a dramatic and integrative approach.

I've included identity pieces as a part of your long-range plan because they are foundational to your outreach into your target market. Invest what you can in them. But before anything, invest your thought into their design and how that design represents you. Get started now and add to your foundation over time.

Research Market

I met Heather Maloy, the Artistic Director of Terpsicorps Theatre of Dance (www.terpsicorps.org) because two of my clients had called my office in one week to say "Find out about that new dance company in town. They cater to our target market." I had to agree. After all, I had seen the posters around town and noticed the amount of press this hot new dance troupe was attracting. My clients who called, wanting me to bridge a connection with Terpsicorps, were interested in attracting a financially high profile, socially responsible audience. My clients had done their research.

Thorough research into your market means answering the following questions:

1. What is my target market? What are their values and roles?

2. Where do they network? Socialize? Form support groups? Worship? Live? Eat? Go to work?

3. What non-competing organizations are already in communication with my target market?

4. What social causes does my target market support? Which ones resonate with my business values and are in need of the strengths I can offer through my role(s) as a community-oriented business?

5. Who is my competition? Where and with whom do they do business? What is their marketing approach? How can I set myself apart?

Start Building Your Network and Establish Contacts

Now that you've done your research and identified your target market, start making the connections that will bring you into the community sphere of which they are a part. When you start networking and building contacts, do so strategically. Don't just look for established networking groups. Look for the movers and shakers in town whose businesses are in your ideal contact sphere.

Your ideal contact sphere is a focused list of professionals who compliment your business but do not compete with it. By complimenting your business, I mean that they serve a similar clientele to yours and come into regular contact with the exact type of person that you are on the lookout for. For example, a massage therapist should network with personal trainers, chiropractors, salon owners and hotel executives. A telephone sales executive should network with commercial real estate developers, relocation companies, property management businesses and corporate law firms.

As you network, remember that you are on the lookout for strategic alliances and relationships that will grow your business. You are also on the lookout for opportunities to get involved in the communities that host your target market. Enact the rules we talked about earlier. Connect openly and without a hungry focus on sales. Make eye contact. Smile. Send thank-you notes to everyone you get a business card from or, when appropriate, send gifts. Book two weeks ahead with daily lunch and coffee appointments. At the end of two weeks, you should have enough data on your plate to keep you busy for a while.

When Heather Maloy and I met for coffee in downtown Asheville, we spent about an hour together, talking about ways in which we could strategically offer each other support. Rather than put in a dry request for her media kit at the calling of my clients, I sent her an email and invited her to meet personally. As a result, we've joined forces to create community awareness events and fundraisers that model the suggestions I made earlier in this book.

Identify Needs and Opportunities to Enact Roles for Community Empowerment

Who needs you? Is it a merchant association? A chamber orchestra? A theater company? A neighborhood? A community center? A networking group? A school? A homeless shelter? A crisis hotline? An animal shelter? An outdoors group? A running club? An environmental protection group? How about City Hall? A struggling chamber of commerce? A hospital? Who needs you? Make a list, check it twice and narrow it down.

Create Your 12 Month
Action Plan

Watch out for the software programs out there for designing and implementing your

12-month marketing plan. Many of them center on "advertising campaigns." And while most software programs can be altered to support a community-oriented approach, I encourage you to create a system of your own. In the last section of this book, we'll talk about organizational systems.

Whatever approach you decide to follow, your long-range marketing action plan should achieve the following:

1. **Map out the next 12 months and define a different major community empowerment focus every 2-3 months.** For example, if you have a volunteer program, change your volunteer focus to a new organization periodically, returning to the best volunteering relationships at the same time each year.

2. **Define ongoing community-oriented marketing-related events and enact a corresponding schedule for communicating with the media.** For example, if you have a free workshop scheduled for the month of June, there should be marketing and press activities during the 6 weeks leading up to that date.

3. **Institute specific activities that occur monthly.** I know a Feng Shui consultant who takes her clients and colleagues hiking once a month. It is an opportunity to provide an emotional and memorable experience, as well as enjoy casual social contact. Another example: my friend who publishes a magazine drives all over town on the first Monday of every month, just stopping in to smile and say hello to every advertiser in her magazine.

4. **Establish specific actions for each day of each week.** For me, Tuesday is networking day. I line up personal meetings and go to networking

groups all day. Wednesday is interpersonal communications day. I send out thank-you notes, select gifts for important prospects, make calls and receive calls from morning until noon. These tasks should be considered sacred in your calendar and never be rescheduled.

5. **Allow breaks.** Sometimes, you have to take a vacation from perpetually focusing on your marketing goals. On a quarterly basis, give yourself a few weeks off from your marketing plan. Then schedule a "check-in" which will allow you to review the past quarter and make adjustments to the one ahead. This practice will give you the distance necessary to have a clear and analytical perspective. It will also help keep you fresh.

6. **Be realistic.** It is just about impossible to plan an entire year ahead and actually stick to the initial plan through to the end. New contacts will arise, new opportunities will present themselves. Make your plan flexible, *but commit to following through with your goals.*

Get excited! Establish clear goals, assess your strengths, create positive roles, research your market and strategically build resources. By taking these actions, you'll rise above 99 % of all other professionals in your field. Less than 1% of all individuals on earth ever take the time to clearly define what they want and then create a tangible plan of realistic actions to make it happen. Congratulations!

"We must be the change that we wish to see in the world"

—Ghandi

PART V
A Few Things You Will Need To Know

Unlocking The Power Of Media

If you overlook this portion of the book, your results will be inconsequential in comparison to traditional marketing. Community-oriented marketing utilizes media as an integrated promotional tool. It is imperative to success, so get to know your local media.

I have a bizarre relationship with the media. While I love information, I dislike a great deal of what is distributed by mainstream outlets. I personally feel that the media spends more time playing on our fears than it spends educating us with relevant information for our daily lives. But the fact is, the media, in all its manifestations, is a tool. In some countries, the media is a tool used primarily by corporations. In others, the media is for the exclusive use of government only. In the United States and much of developed Europe, media policy and image-makers are reinventing daily the role their industry plays to accommodate for 3 major opinions they have experienced.

1. The media is losing credibility.

2. The media is too liberal.

3. The media is too conservative.

A dramatic re-organization of the media has matured. While your parents were likely to have read the same magazines as neighbors with whom they had little in common, your children will take in media that is prepared and delivered especially for them. From Women's Business Journals to The History Channel, the media has learned that knowing its audience creates more interest in its product from the market that it wishes to target. Add into this mix the introductions of internet communication, digital processing technology and desktop publishing, all of which have helped bring about an overload of information and a saturation of professional media organizations. There are more magazines and newspapers in the United States alone than there were magazines and newspapers on the *entire* planet 100 years ago—and, significantly, the majority of these publications are specialized and target-marketed.

The purpose of this section is to ease the state of overwhelm which many marketers face when deciding what media to include in their marketing and public relations. The first thing I encourage you to do is shrink the playing field and focus only on the outlets that will produce strong results. From a community-oriented marketing perspective, you can usually reduce your options down to less than a dozen.

Just keep in mind, as you narrow the field, that there are two relationships with the media that you must address:

1. Advertising

2. Getting Press

So let's take a summarized tour of today's metropolitan media, with a focus on getting press.

A Brief Review of Urban Media

In an urban setting, you can easily create a list of 40-100 potential media outlets for your message. Before you make any decisions, I encourage marketers to sit down and compile a realistic list of the media best-positioned to deliver directly to your target market.

Mainstream Newspapers:

Despite subscriber decline throughout the past decade, daily papers of all kinds remain one of the best ways to get information out to the general public and business community.

Local TV:

Television caters to a general audience. Local TV news coverage which promotes your business is priceless and should be considered essential to a long range public relations plan.

CABLE TV:

Because cable companies are required to have a local access channel, many businesses have learned that they can open the door to a local viewing audience with far less effort than with other stations. Cities vary dramatically from one to the next in terms of how seriously the public takes their local access.

LOCAL MAGAZINES & NEWSPAPERS:

Our cities are practically bombarded by local magazines these days and I love it. What better way to target the ideal local customer? There is only one challenge—which one do you use in order to target your ideal market? Before you advertise in a single local magazine or paper, call them up and ask that they mail you a media kit. Their media kit should include demographical data about their reader base, distribution areas, etc.

RADIO

It is tough to get press on radio stations that focus on music and traffic reports. But depending on your audience, radio can be the strongest or weakest link in a media campaign. Talk radio and public radio are known for their "active listening" audience and I usually put them at the top of any release distribution list.

ELECTRONIC MEDIA:

Email Newsletters, Web News Communities, E-Zines and Web Radio all have their benefits and limitations. Some work well; others are a terrible waste of energy. Just like other forms of media, the key is to do your research. The most efficient electronic media outlets are those produced by established communities with an active audience. For example, when I was a software engineer many years ago, the place to be was a website called www.developer.com. There, intermediate programmers such as I could gain insights from the old pros. Ours was a community of smart people who were hungry for information. When the newsletter would hit my email box, I usually read it within a day or so. On the other hand, 80% of all newsletters that arrive in my email get trashed right away. How do you choose the right one(s)? I suggest talking to your colleagues in your industry. They usually will be quick to share answers.

TRADE JOURNALS & ASSOCIATION PERIODICALS:

The majority of all distinct industries and associations have magazines and newspapers that keep their community up to date about what is going on within that industry or association. Most of them are national, but lately we've seen a rise in locally focused trade journals and association periodicals. This is an important niche that should inspire you to ask the question: Does a significant portion of my target market belong to one of these industry-related readership communities?

LOCAL NICHE MEDIA

Here's a commonly made mistake—marketers who overlook local niche publications. Neighborhood newspapers, employee newsletters for larger businesses, business-to-business and business-to-customer newspapers, educational & institutional periodicals are the first that come to mind.

THINK LOCAL AND NARROW YOUR FOCUS

As we explore creating media opportunities in greater depth, we'll talk about the buzz of starting your own media outlet. We'll also discuss the do's and don'ts. But as a forethought—if you are going to spend thousands of dollars getting into a publication, it may not be a bad idea to start up a publication of your own. Whether you are spinning off a monthly, 2-page newsletter or a mainstream magazine with a regional focus, there can be a lot of power in new media.

The buzzword in community-oriented marketing is "local." As I mentioned before, your job is to be an expert in your field and a hero in the community. Do the media know this about you? Whatever it is you are doing, the media needs to know about you and trust you as an authority whom they can call upon at any time. In order for this to happen, you must focus on distinguishing yourself from the competition around you. And, of course, one of the best ways to do this is to narrow your own focus and cater to a specific community.

How To Write And Submit A Media Release

So you want to get a story out and you believe it to be press-worthy. If you are reading this book, you are most likely going to be writing your own press release. This is one of the most intimidating prospects for many marketers, and yet, it is really quite simple. Here are some straight-forward pointers:

Journalists want to know who you are, what you're doing, when you're doing it, where it will be and why they should care:

1. Who

2. What

3. When

4. Where

5. Why

These are the core questions behind all journalism—if you don't address them, you are likely to not get press. Don't focus on being smart or funny. Just state the news and state it well. Your prospective journalist will decide within one paragraph of your release whether they consider your story to be newsworthy or not.

Make Sure Your Message Is Attractive To The Media

Of the 5 questions mentioned, the most important one for getting press is the "why." Why do you think that your story or your activity is worthy of press?

By far one of my favorite clients of all time is Asheville Chiropractor Dr. Patrick McMahon. When Patrick called me up and asked how he could get involved with an educational organization that really empowers young people, the first person that came to mind was Derek Croley. Patrick had already supported the City Schools Foundation and other similar organizations whose base includes families (a major part of his target market). But he wanted especially to get involved in the lives of young people who held themselves to higher standards of achievement. Derek Croley, head instructor at Croley's Martial Arts Center, carries a similar vision, the only difference being that he acts as a catalyst. Croley spent most of his life studying peak performance and philosophy. His impact on children as a Martial Arts teacher amazes me. He teaches them the importance of responsibility, self-discipline and community. For example, in order to excel in the belt system at Croley's Martial Arts Center, you must, for each belt advancement, perform a predetermined number of hours volunteering in the community. Here is an excerpt from the end portion of the press release:

> Dr. McMahon chose to endow the Center for the Martial Arts on Charlotte Street in Asheville, considered one of the several finest martial arts schools in the region with the funds to charter a youth scholarship program. McMahon says he selected Center for the Martial Arts because its principal/teacher, Derek Croley, is renowned for teaching applied spiritual principles as an explicit, integrated part of early martial arts training, unlike most instructors who delay this until students master much higher levels of physical technique. Croley's students are noted for being able to gracefully balance their social, academic, athletic and spiritual lives. They are, in short, the kind of young people considered ideal in chiropractic, martial arts and society as a whole: well-adjusted—young people, who, when confronted with the dizzying menu choices in the world's café, choose life.

Any chiropractor reading this book will nod in agreement when I share that chiropractors are some of the toughest professionals in America to market, while staying true to the founding principles of the chiropractic practice. Dr. McMahon shares the ideals of so many other chiropractors I have met, in that he has no interest in operating a revolving door back pain clinic. Finding a way to get the attention of the media for him presented a marketing challenge. A press release announcing the opening of Dr. Pat's office would not have yielded any press. Nor would an announcement pertaining to his involvement in a typical non-profit fundraiser or community event. Getting press for Patrick meant stepping out of the box. The end result of our creative pairing: a marketing/publicity coup.

Many of us have our reservations about the media—reservations that are well-grounded. There are significant challenges to getting our stories noticed. One problem today is that, unfortunately, even news media coverage is now being bought and sold. The fact is, big advertisers are often more likely to get press for their activities in the community than are non-advertisers. Another problem is that the press is inundated daily with garbage proposals (or, great press ideas written so poorly that the effort was wasted), making it tougher for journalists to scout out the gems. But when that feature story or even an editorial mention hits the press, our businesses can change overnight. Depending on your audience, a radio or local evening news interview could be all you need to launch your business to the next level. The question then that, no doubt, looms in every small businessperson's mind is, "How do I get through all of the fluff and grab the attention of the person who calls the shots?" Like everything else in this field, there are 9 wrong ways for every 1 right way to communicate with the media.

Here are the top six considerations when preparing a media release:

1. Answer the five questions: who, what, when, where and why.

2. Give the media a reason to care. Make sure that what you are sending them appeals to their reader base and will get lots of attention.

3. Carefully use a newsworthy quote, alliance or tie-in for your press efforts. Get a recognized name involved. Has your local mayor said anything quotable which indicates a possible demand for a solution to a problem—a solution which is provided by your product? Who else can you tie into your media release? At the same time, be careful: the media hates name-dropping. Don't use a recognized name to build up an otherwise dull release. Use it, instead, to empower an outstanding one.

4. Make sure that your release promotes an activity or product which is instrumental in improving the quality of life for a recognized community in your city.

5. Keep it to one page and one page only. I know journalists who discard multi-page press releases without even reading them. If you can't make your point in one page, your story is likely too complicated for them to research and produce press for.

6. Check your calendar and plan press releases carefully. All media experience story lags and smart businesses will jump on them. Vacation season, specifically the month of August, is best for summertime releases. The week leading up to Christmas, and those weeks continuing on through the month of January, are also typically slow times.

GETTING YOUR RELEASE OUT TO THE PRESS

Make a goal of getting to know your journalists in town. Get a list of who covers what section/topic/editorial focus for every publication you wish to be involved in. Read them. Scan for articles of other businesses in action for inspiration on what might be press-worthy for your own. Think forward. Don't try to copycat stories that have already run. Instead, think about what is *not* being covered that is applicable to each publication's reader demands. Send out at least one press release per month on entirely different subjects and endeavors. Don't repeat the same idea with a creative rewrite. If your release doesn't get press, move on to the next one in one month's time.

As for submissions, you can mail, email and fax your release in.

1. Mail: Many media outlets still prefer mail, so cover this base every time. When mailing a press release, include a CD-Rom with relevant high-resolution images and attention it to the individual who is responsible for reporting on your topic.

2. Email: Depending on your publication, email may be the best way to go. If you are unable to locate email addresses for the appropriate department, just phone the publication and ask them what is best. Provided that they do accept email submissions, make sure that your subject line is alluring. Don't say "Press release attached" or "Widgets R Us Announcement." Instead, create a line from the body of your release that compels the recipient to actually double click on your email.

3. Fax: While it makes sense to cover all bases, many media outlets have become disenchanted with the fax machine. There are even media outlets that have set up their fax lines as 900 charge-by-minute services to dissuade faxed releases. At the same time, you never know. Some publications love a faxed release. So before you fax, call and ask. They are always happy to tell you their preferred method of submission.

You can also get someone else to do it for you. Newswire services do an excellent job and will often even write your release for an additional charge. The best company for this, in my experience, is Business Wire (www.businesswire.com). These companies also handle video & multimedia broadcast releases. The fee, depending on quantity and geographic focus, usually ranges up to several hundred dollars for regular releases.

Organization—Create A System For Follow-up And Stick To It

Do yourself a favor. Go pick up a great book by David Allen entitled *Getting Things Done*. In it, Allen goes deep into the nature of our complex business lives and identifies the major obstacles we face in managing sound organizational systems. He then provides a "Get it out of your head" approach to stress-free productivity that is easy to follow and creates measurable results.

In addition, while no program is holistic for organizing a community-oriented marketing plan, I suggest that you choose a software or web-based project management program that works for you. You may even want to hire a database programmer to visit your office and create one customized for your business. It all depends on the complexity of your marketing plan.

But the most important organizational system you can create—one that will enable the smooth growth of your business—is a contacts management system. Figure 4.1 is a rough diagram of what you'll need to juggle. An organizational record-keeping system is an essential aspect of your community—oriented marketing plan. This system for keeping track of contacts should be focused not on warehousing data but on committing to a routine follow-up schedule. It should achieve the following:

1. Your contacts management system should act as a "one-stop-shop" for as much information as you can collect about every individual you meet. This includes:

    *   Who referred you to them

    *   What business they are associated with and what they do

    *   What community groups they are associated with

    *   What resources you can gain from them for future reference

    *   What resources you can offer them

    *   Where you met them

2. It should keep track of dates and circumstances of all follow-ups associated with this contact.

- When you met them

- When their birthday is and how old they are

- When you sent a thank-you note or greeting card to them

- When you call, write letters or otherwise communicate with them (please note that if you speak with someone daily or even weekly, this kind of data is less relevant). Whatever the circumstances, be personal. Take the time to really care.

- The most important thing to remember is that for optimum results, enact your encore at least once every 3 months.

Project under-management, like projects executed from an old legal pad with a ballpoint pen, will serve against you in community-oriented marketing. Just as business has grown more complex, getting the most out of community activities has grown more challenging. This means thinking deeper and seeking creative ways to maximize results. These creative ways of interconnecting your marketing efforts work, but they will also typically complicate what on the surface, looked like a simple event.

Ideally, then, your contact management system should serve you as an integral part of your long-range marketing plan. And your marketing plan should be well defined as a time-managed system (see figure 4.2). For each project which involves an event, you also need to create an organizational system (see figure 4.3). For example, if you put The Encore into action as a weekly practice, then you will be able to populate any event you get involved with by leveraging those contacts alone. Incorporating your contacts management system with your marketing plan will make planning events easier as well. You'll be able to leverage resources by finding service providers through your network, rather than by looking in the phone book. You'll have a destination for every press release from every community project you promote. Given recent changes in technology and business needs, it's now possible to accurately plan and schedule a multiple-month project up front. Delivering functionality every week, even if that functionality is determined by a phone call, will help keep even the longest of projects on track. This approach also helps to keep your customers involved throughout the process since they can see results each week.

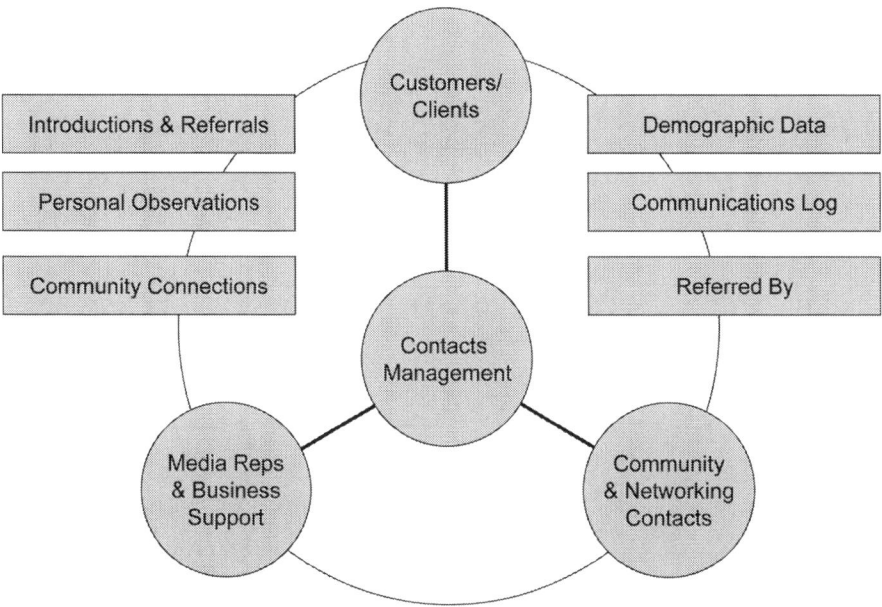

Figure 4.1 Contact Organizational Overview

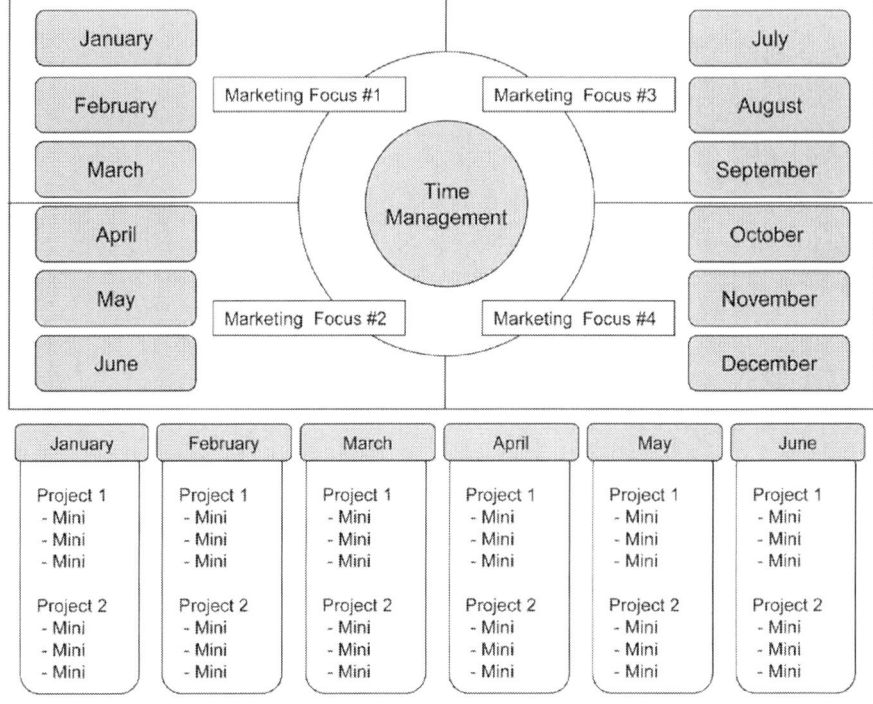

Figure 4.2 Time Management Organizational Overview

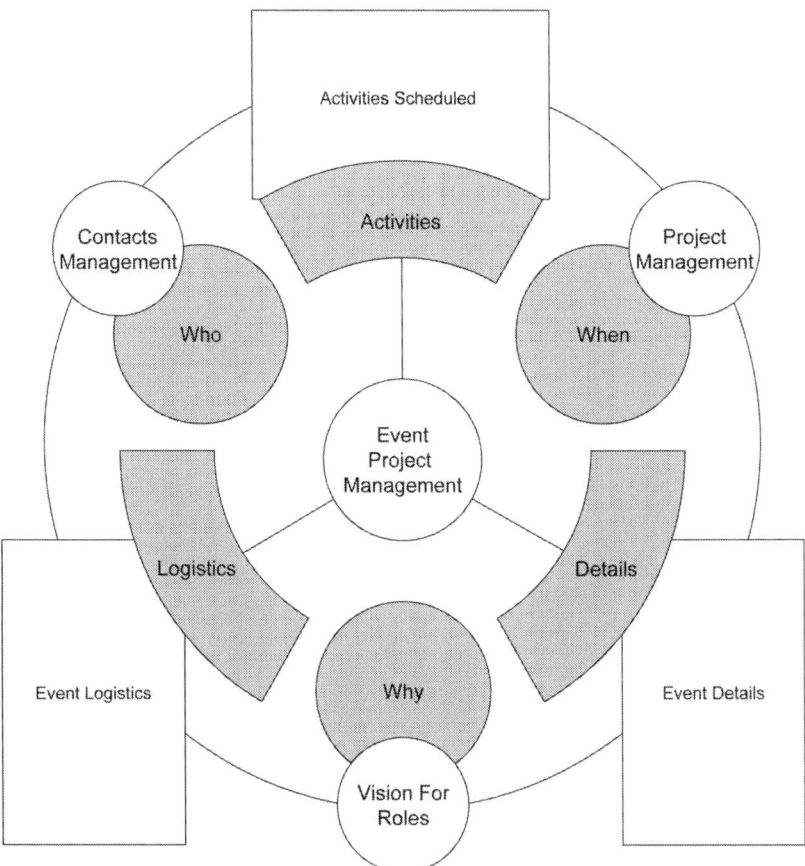

Figure 4.3 Event Management Organizational Overview

Play Full Out—Transforming Disappointments Into Achievements

When I was in high school, I remember that our football coach would always talk about playing "Full Out." "Come on ladies," he would yell. "Play full out! I want to see one hundred and ten percent on that field! I want to see you rip the grass from the soil!"

Thank goodness I survived high school without getting expelled for strangling him. But many years later, I was at a seminar where the speaker asked the group to "Play Full Out." It was the first time I had heard the term since those awkward days in high school, so he got my full attention. He wrote it in large letters on the dry erase board. He then told the audience, "Turn off your analytical mind and forget about what you know. Then open your mind to that which is possible. We will present some new ideas that have the potential to change your life. At the end of the day, you can do or think whatever you want. But for the purpose of getting the most value for your investment, I ask that everyone here *play full out*."

That presenter was Alan Brown of Anthony Robbins & Associates, Inc. in Chicago. I played "full out" that day and I've attempted to do so every day of my adult life since. Playing full out in community-oriented marketing is about holding yourself to the highest possible standards of professional conduct. It is about taming your ego while assuming confidence. It is about making eye contact and smiling when you meet people. It is about giving twice as much as you ever expect to receive. And most importantly, it is about staying positive, constructive and pro-active in all of your endeavors.

Here is my top ten list for playing full out:

1. Never spread rumors or talk about people behind their backs. It is not a question of *if* in today's interconnected world. It is a question of *when* it will come back to bite you.

2. Connect. Always pay close attention to others and listen more than you talk.

3. Tell the truth whenever possible.

4. Assume responsibility for every situation that falls under your sphere of control. Never blame or pass judgment.

5. Every day, brainstorm ways in which you can empower others. Each and every action will come back to you in due time.

6. Always look for ways to take your involvement in the community to a higher level.

7. Always look for the lesson in "failures." In fact, don't use the world failure at all. Recognize that some things just don't work and keep changing your approach until you get where you want to go.

8. Be grateful. Never accept anything without giving due thanks.

9. Give gifts of attention, compassion and information. Educate people if they are open. Let them know that you want to help them with specific information.

10. Find out when people celebrate their birthdays and don't just send a card…call them and sing "Happy Birthday" into their voicemail.

When you meet someone and they ask you how you are doing, don't answer "Just fine, thanks." Try something more along the lines of "I am having a wonderful day, thank you for asking. And yourself?" Turn on. Pay attention. Remember names. Be compassionate. And always ask yourself what you can do to improve the lives of others. Don't focus on what you can get out of others; instead, focus on what you can give.

Disappointments will come. I promise you that as you follow this path for your business development, you will enact unfruitful marketing activities that may cost you money. Turn it around. Make each disappointment into a research project. Keep it in perspective. Remember that if you were following a traditional marketing approach, it would likely cost more than your typical small loss in community-oriented marketing.

But there is another reason to play full out. With the best attitude in town, guess what: You provide a memorable, emotionally compelling experience to each person you interact with. We all know how nice it feels to talk with someone who feels like a million bucks. Why not be one of those people? Your business can orchestrate the perfect introduction and even deliver an ideal experience. But if your prospect doesn't experience a positive rush of good vibes from you, you could lose the sale.

It is our responsibility as professionals to make business fun and interesting. As a community-oriented businessperson, you'll probably notice that good deeds and good people are contagious. So, play full out. Along the way, you may even learn something about yourself.

Going Grassroots—Getting Results On A Shoestring Budget

Low-budget marketing *can be* risky, no matter how you look at it. But community-oriented marketing *is* low-budget marketing. So, while you can spend as much as you like, community-oriented marketing proves to be the most effective low-budget approach. The previous section, which listed 18 community-oriented marketing techniques, offers many low and even a few no-budget marketing ideas. There are certainly more. When I owned a coffeehouse business in Chicago's Wicker Park, my manager would rent a chicken costume and run up and down the street during rush hour with a giant cup in her chicken hand. She would pass out coupons to the public emerging from the blue-line subway stop. It generated a fantastic response. At other times, we would have a thin cow stand outside next to the sidewalk tables and pass out "skinny latte" promotions to passers by. All it really cost us was the costume rentals, which we made up in coffee sales. Is that community-oriented marketing? Only if you consider my contribution to the street scene a community asset! But it worked. So if you are marketing on a budget, pick up other bang-for-buck marketing books and feel free to integrate. Just make sure that every marketing project is in line with your stated values.

These days, for most businesses, choosing the best budget-on-a-shoestring marketing tactics is like going shopping in a megamall. There are always several dozen options. The question is, which options are right for your business? It's very hard for many marketers to separate the best from the rest. So make sure that your budget marketing project:

- reaches your target market and communicates your values and professionalism

- communicates directly and effectively to your community

- can be combined or expanded to cooperate with other marketing projects

129

Every effective marketing strategy, including the low-budget variety, allows for a call to action. For some activities, this simply means including a web address on a printed piece. For public appearance marketing tactics, this means offering a contest or holding a drawing. Whatever your direction, make sure that you compel an immediate action or response. For an integrative program, combine your sales approach with your marketing tactics. Track your responses by "bring in this ad" terminology or by offering coupons and project-specific discounts.

Whatever you do, please be tasteful and considerate in your efforts to market on a limited budget. Avoid spending two hundred dollars to print a flyer that looks like a 4th-grader designed it. When talking with other business owners and negotiating services, try not to mention the fact that you are barely scraping out the meager budget you have to work with. Remember that your graphic designer deserves to make a living just as much as you do, so appreciate the value of what people display as their asking price. If you wish to "talk down" a printer, advertising outlet or any other business which is helping you with your marketing, *be respectful*. If you ask for a bargain basement price, expect bargain basement results. Instead, ask them what opportunities there are for you to reduce the price without being rude.

I chose to talk about low-budget marketing at the end of the book because my hope is that the content of the book leading up to the conclusion makes this point on its own. It is important to understand, however, that the more money you can muster up to spend on your marketing, the better. While there are many books out there about brilliant marketing ideas that make millions of dollars for almost no money—the truth is that these are hard to come by. So if you have the money to spend, spend it and spend it well. And remember—what usually makes the difference between success and failure in marketing is you—your integrity, compassion and positive attitude.

"Appreciation is a wonderful thing: It makes what is excellent in others belong to us as well."

—Voltaire

Conclusion

I hope that this information has inspired you the way inspires me. When clients call my office out of the blue, beaming about how successful their businesses have become, I get excited because I feel great confidence about the impact that this kind of business has on our future. I know about the personal growth which so many community-oriented marketers experience. I know what it is like to be a contributing part of something greater than oneself—something that enriches the lives of so many people. This method of business development will ultimately spread throughout the globe because it is what most of us really want to see happen. And that's why I wrote this book…to reach out and make an example of these champions I work with every day whose businesses represent these community-oriented marketing principles.

Let's face it: in most capitalistic economies, business runs the backstage show. Businesses influences government, which, in turn, relies upon them to fund its operation, build its societies and employ its people. Our governments are usually too busy to organize the random public into an intentional league of progressive visionaries with an agenda. This is an action we have to take for ourselves. That's why we tested the waters and found a way to make community-oriented marketing work in any developed city on earth.

Here is my dream. I hope that you can help me make it into a reality. I want to see 100 businesses in your hometown market themselves by using these tools. Considering the fact that there are at least dozens of businesses in every city that are already following these principles, this dream is easy to fulfill. There is no set number, but most of my clients spend between $12,000 and $150,000 per year on marketing. I believe that this range represents most small businesses that are serious about growth. So ask yourself, "What would it mean for my city if one hundred businesses were spending one thousand dollars per month that went primarily towards community empowerment activities?"

It would mean over a million dollars of new revenue in your city alone for community development. It would mean a safer, cleaner, more educated and well-fed society than ever before…right outside of your front door. It would also cultivate more volunteers, more awareness about socially responsible business and more media that is sensitive to businesses which choose to get involved. And here is the best part…anyone can be a part of this equation. Even the simplest home-based family businesses out there can benefit dramatically from getting involved at the ground level.

While I have your attention, I would like to ask you a personal favor. If you work with youth, please investigate the *Roots & Shoots Program* that is available all over the world. This community based program sets a foundation for members (K-University) to participate as individuals, in groups and as part of a global network. In local groups, Roots & Shoots members plan and carryout projects based on their group's unique interests, resources and community concerns. Roots & Shoots projects address one or more of the following three themes:

- Care and concern for the environment
- Care and concern for animals
- Care and concern for the human community

To learn more about Roots & Shoots, contact The Jane Goodall Institute at www.janegoodall.org. There are many more national and international organizations which are active on local levels as cornerstones of community empowerment. I suggest that you do your research and find the best ones which will allow you to support the community while the community, in turn, supports your business.

Let me know how it goes. Send an email to ianbryan@community-oriented.com with your stories, feedback and questions. Visit the website if you are looking for more insights, ideas or resources for your own community-oriented marketing plan. And please, if you have been influenced by this book, share it with a friend. Thank you.

Ian Bryan
Asheville, North Carolina

Suggested Reading

1. *Reason For Hope*, Dr. Jane Goodall

2. *The Rise Of The Creative Class*, Richard Florida

3. *Good Business*, Mihaly Csikszentmihalyi

4. *Love Is The Killer App*, Tim Sanders

5. *The Experience Economy*, Gilmore & Pine

6. *Attracting Perfect Customers*, Hall & Brogniez

7. *Re-imagine!*, Tom Peters

8. *Off The Wall Marketing Ideas*, Michaels & Karpowicz

9. *Bowling Alone*, Robert Putnam

10. *The Tipping Point*, Malcolm Gladwell

11. *1001 Ways To Market Your Services*, Rick Crandall

12. *Permission Marketing*, Seth Godin

13. *Competition In The 21st Century*, Kirk Tyson

New Magazines

1. *Hope Magazine (www.hopemag.com)*

2. *The Next American City (www.americancity.org)*

About The Author

Ian Bryan teaches city-based professionals how to break free from the expensive, unpredictable and insensitive marketing ecosystem which dominates today's business world. He is the Chief Executive and Founder of The Sensible City, the first marketing agency in the world to focus on purely community-oriented business development and marketing.

Ian is a native Tennessean who spent the better part of the "internet bubble" era as CEO of New Human, Inc. out of Chicago, Illinois. In 1999, New Human reshaped its focus to support primarily community oriented business, working with local city governments, performing arts troupes, endangered species and human services firms. While managing operations at New Human, Ian also served as Executive V.P. of Support Services for Siteleader.com, Inc.

In the spring of 2001, wanting to expand into more community-centered business development, Ian created Sensible City with the vision of connecting businesses with the communities that support them. A former coffee house owner, professional athlete and skydiver, Ian loves a challenge and has been known to bring his mountaineering skills to the drawing board. He lives with his family in Asheville, North Carolina.

Printed in Great Britain
by Amazon